# 10-MINUTE

# DECLUTTER

# 10-MINUTE

# DECLUTTER

Hundreds of Tips to Organize Every
Room of Your House

WRITTEN BY

## SKYE ALEXANDER

FAIR WINDS

Brimming with creative inspiration, how-to projects, and useful information to enrich your everyday life, Quarto Knows is a favorite destination for those pursuing their interests and passions. Visit our site and dig deeper with our books into your area of interest: Quarto Creates, Quarto Cooks, Quarto Homes, Quarto Lives, Quarto Drives, Quarto Explores, Quarto Gifts, or Quarto Kids.

First Published in 2019 by Fair Winds Press, an imprint of The Quarto Group, 100 Cummings Center, Suite 265-D, Beverly, MA 01915, USA.
T (978) 282-9590 F (978) 283-2742 QuartoKnows.com

Fair Winds Press titles are also available at discount for retail, wholesale, promotional, and bulk purchase. For details, contact the Special Sales Manager by email at specialsales@quarto.com or by mail at The Quarto Group, Attn: Special Sales Manager, 100 Cummings Center, Suite 265-D, Beverly, MA 01915, USA.

23 22 21 20 19      1 2 3 4 5

ISBN: 978-1-59233-914-3

Digital edition published in 2019
eISBN: 978-1-63159-816-6

This content appeared in the previously published book *10-Minute Clutter Control* by Skye Alexander (Fair Winds Press, 2004).

Library of Congress Cataloging-in-Publication Data under *10-Minute Clutter Control*.

Design, page layout, and illustrations: Tanya Jacobson, crsld.co

Printed in China

TO MY NEAT AND
ORDERLY SISTER, MYKE,
WITH GRATITUDE
FOR HER CONSTANT
ENCOURAGEMENT.

# Contents

# *Introduction*

When I first started using feng shui (pronounced *fung shway*), few people in the West had heard of it. Today, scores of English-language books and articles have been written on the subject. You can buy feng shui candles, feng shui cosmetics, feng shui refrigerator magnets, feng shui greeting cards, and a host of other products that may or may not have any real value or any genuine relationship to this ancient Chinese art.

Yet there's still a lot of confusion about feng shui. What are the core concepts? Do you have to completely redo your home according to feng shui principles, or can you benefit from making just a few updates?

Like experts in medicine, religion, golf, or any other field, feng shui practitioners subscribe to different theories and come to different understandings over time as a result of their own experiences. One thing just about everyone agrees on, however, is that clutter must be controlled. If you implement only one feng shui cure, get rid of the dirt, debris, and damage in your home.

*10-Minute Declutter* expands on some of the ideas from my book *10-Minute Feng Shui*. It looks at the deeper significance of clutter in our homes and workplaces, how this affects us, and how we can remove obstacles in our lives simply by cleaning up the clutter around us.

# HOW TO USE THIS BOOK

*10-Minute Declutter* focuses on one essential feng shui cure—getting rid of clutter. Cures, by the way, are techniques designed to produce certain effects or to eliminate unwanted ones. In Part One, I explain the ABCs of feng shui and why it works. I also discuss the symbolism and psychology of clutter and how you can eliminate problems in your life by eliminating clutter in your environment.

Part Two contains tips and solutions for clearing away clutter. These tips are grouped into five categories: home, workplace, areas outside your home, kids, and your personal life. Many can be implemented in ten minutes or so. The other, larger tasks, such as cleaning out an attic or basement, can be broken down into small segments to make them more manageable.

If you don't want to know much about feng shui, you can go directly to Part Two and get started. But if you're the sort of person who likes to understand *why* as well as *how*, Part One explains why making changes in your living and work areas will change your life.

The most important factor in successfully using feng shui is your intent—the physical cures are only part of the process. You'll get better results if you truly want to correct a particular problem and if you believe that what you are doing will work. In this sense, feng shui is a lot like other endeavors—the more you put into it, the more you get back.

# PART
# ONE

# Understanding Feng Shui in Your Life

CH

1

# THE BASICS OF
# FENG SHUI

Western society tends to think of luck as pure chance. The people who follow the ancient Chinese practice of feng shui, however, believe we can cultivate and manipulate luck. Rather than simply playing the hand Fate dealt them in the game of life, they use this method to remedy their problems and attract health, wealth, and happiness.

Feng shui's objective is to create harmony and balance in your environment. To accomplish this, feng shui masters apply a variety of practical solutions, called *cures*, to everyday problems. These remedies include such things as establishing convenient traffic patterns through your home, positioning furniture in comfortable arrangements, and eliminating clutter in your living and work spaces. There's nothing magical about these cures—they are sensible ways to make life easier and more efficient.

But feng shui also has a mystical component based on the *I Ching*, ancient Chinese philosophy, color and number symbolism, and other esoteric knowledge. Many of the cures feng shui recommends are symbolic as well as practical. The logical solutions enable you to function more effectively and comfortably; the symbolic ones influence your subconscious to change old patterns and conditioned responses that may be blocking you at a deeper level.

## The Art of Placement

Feng shui is also known as the art of placement. By placing furniture, accessories, artworks, architectural elements, personal objects, and so on in particular spots, you create either a comfortable environment that people enjoy spending time in or an unpleasant one they can't wait to leave. Many good interior designers and architects unconsciously understand the principles of feng shui and use them automatically to create harmonious, well-balanced environments.

Even if you've never studied feng shui or interior design, you've undoubtedly experienced the effects of good and bad placement. For instance, if the first thing you encountered upon entering a living room was the back of a sofa, how would you feel? Unwelcome? Blocked? If you walked into an office and saw clutter everywhere, what would you think? That the person who worked there was so busy or distracted that he or she might not be able to pay attention to you? Once you start noticing your feelings and responses when you enter a space, you'll begin to understand how feng shui works.

## Ch'i: Feng Shui's Pulse of Life

Literally translated, *feng shui* means *wind* and *water*. Wind and water, as we know, can be harnessed to produce energy. Feng shui also allows us to control and direct natural forces and utilize their energy constructively.

The principal force feng shui considers is *ch'i* (pronounced *chee*), the life-giving energy of the Universe that flows through everything—our homes, the Earth, our bodies. Acupuncturists use needles to eliminate blockages so ch'i can move freely in the body. Feng shui practitioners employ various cures, such as those discussed in Part Two, to keep ch'i flowing smoothly through our environments. One of the most common impediments to ch'i in our homes and workplaces is clutter. Clearing clutter from your environment is like unclogging a pipe so water can run through it again.

Ch'i travels through an area in much the same way you do. As you walk about your home, notice whether the pathways you normally use are easy to navigate or obstructed. Do they invite you to enter? Is it difficult to move through the space or to open windows and doors? Do some areas feel pleasant, others awkward or uncomfortable? You can't see ch'i, but after you work with it a while, you'll begin to sense its presence.

Ideally, you want ch'i to move through a space like a gently flowing stream or a light breeze. If it rushes by too quickly, it won't have time to bestow its life-giving benefits. If it gets "stuck" and sits like a stagnant pool, you may feel uneasy or even become physically ill. Clutter, debris, dirt, and disrepair interfere with the healthy flow of ch'i, producing tension, confusion, stuffiness, congestion, and a general feeling of malaise. Once clutter has been cleared away, other feng shui cures, such as lights, plants, sound, color, and mirrors, can be employed to rectify ch'i imbalances and create harmonious environments in which to live and work.

## As Within, So Without

Our homes clearly demonstrate this axiom—so clearly that a feng shui master can walk through your home and see at a glance what's going on in your career, your family, your love life. From the point of view of feng shui, your home says a great deal about you—not only about your taste, but also which areas of your life are stable and balanced and which ones are incomplete, obstructed, or unsettled.

That's because your home is a symbol of you—the outer representation of your inner state. This powerful symbol not only reveals what's taking place in every area of your life, but it also shows your attitudes toward your situation. How you furnish, decorate, clean, and arrange your living space express in visual terms what's going on inside you—whether or not you are aware of it.

Here's an example. A woman I used to know was very private and refused to let many people get close to her. Her home, although large and well appointed, was so cluttered that there was no place to sit—a clear reflection of her reluctance to welcome visitors.

Take a good look at your own living space. If you're like most people, you'll notice that some areas are neat, clean, and orderly, while others are messy or neglected. Are your social areas inviting but your study chaotic? A feng shui practitioner might interpret this as an indication that you enjoy friendship and entertaining but find work less appealing. Perhaps you've been meaning to organize or do repairs in a certain sector of your home but never seem to get around to it. These disorderly parts correspond to unresolved issues in your life that you don't want to confront.

In chapter 3, I'll show you how to analyze your home to spot problems. Then, in chapter 4, I'll explain how you can fix your life by fixing your home.

## Intention

The physical parts of feng shui can't be separated from the psychological ones. When you implement a cure—such as repositioning furniture, installing adequate lighting, or cleaning up clutter—you show that you want to improve conditions in your life by improving the condition of your environment. Once you decide you are ready for a change, you'll just naturally start applying feng shui cures in your home and workplace.

Your intention to take charge of your life and create your own luck is the most important part of feng shui. In a sense, your willpower is the active ingredient in feng shui, the power that makes it work.

Although feng shui cures will have an impact even if your heart isn't in it, you'll get better results if you are purposeful in what you do. If you lack sincerity or perform the cures without really intending to change your life, you may lapse back into old habits—such as allowing clutter to pile up again—and nullify the positive benefits of the cures you applied.

CH

2

# THE PROBLEM
# WITH CLUTTER

A lbert Einstein may not have known anything about feng shui, but his opinions on clutter control suggest he understood its basic concepts when he said, "Out of clutter, find simplicity. From discord, find harmony. In the middle of difficulty, lies opportunity."

Much of feng shui involves symbolic associations. Physical conditions in our environments symbolize emotional issues and attitudes we hold. Broken furniture, for instance, can signify broken dreams, physical injuries, or a breakdown in communication among family members. Dirty windows make it difficult to see situations clearly. Doors or drawers that stick may represent aspects of your life that are stuck.

It's easy to see the connection between physical clutter and messiness in your personal life. We even use the term "baggage" to describe old concepts, hang-ups, and behaviors that limit personal growth and happiness. If an area in your home is cluttered, you are probably experiencing confusion or blockages in the part of your life that corresponds to the cluttered section. Conversely, areas that you just naturally tend to keep neat and organized show the parts of your life that function smoothly. (I'll talk more about this in the next chapter.)

I have a friend whose home is extremely neat—except the area that's linked with love and relationships. This room is full of empty bottles and boxes, old paint cans, cast-off furniture, and cartons of memorabilia from his youth (including photo albums containing pictures of old girlfriends). The room has no heat and the roof leaks. No one who understands feng shui would be surprised to learn that this man has a lot of unresolved issues and outdated attitudes about women, love, and relationships.

Large-scale clutter produces physical obstacles that indicate the presence of psychological obstacles. The home of another man I know is cluttered with enormous piles of stuff. Books and magazines, clothing, DVDs, dishes, electrical equipment, athletic gear, and more are stacked on top of furniture. It's almost as if he has built a "clutter fortress."

Many people who have experienced poverty hold on to stuff they may not need because—consciously or not—they fear the shortages they experienced earlier in life. Holding on to old stuff, however, can keep you from letting go of the past and moving ahead with your life.

From the perspective of feng shui, clutter can represent several things:

- Confusion: Disarray and disorganization in your environment show that some areas of your life are messy or unsettled.

- Old baggage: Saving old and worn-out or unused items suggests that you are holding on to old ideas, attitudes, grudges, fears, or habits and allowing them to clutter your psyche.

- Obstacles: Piles of stuff represent blocks that limit your progress; they physically hamper your movement and hinder the flow of ch'i through your environment.

By clearing away the physical clutter around you, you can actually clear up disorder and difficulties in your life—sometimes overnight!

# CLUTTER, DIRT, AND DISREPAIR

From the perspective of feng shui, it's advantageous to free your home of clutter, dirt, and disrepair. Some homes are plagued by all three, while others may suffer from only one. That's because each of these problems symbolizes something different.

Clutter refers to an accumulation of too much stuff, without proper organization or distinction. Clutter usually signifies confusion, lack of focus, chaos, instability, or muddled circumstances. If your home is cluttered, you may have too much going on and lack direction or a sense of priorities. Perhaps you are scattering your energy, rather than dedicating yourself to what's really important. You may be uncertain about your goals, who you are, or what you want in life. Often we see this sort of clutter in teenagers' rooms because they haven't sorted out these personal matters yet.

Dirt suggests low self-esteem, a low energy level, or poor health. Animals often stop cleaning themselves when they are sick or under stress. The same thing happens with people. If you lack vitality or enthusiasm for life, you may not see the value in cleaning your home. If your sense of self-worth is poor, you may not feel you deserve to live in pleasant surroundings. Do you know people who always apologize for the unsightly condition of their home? These people are actually apologizing for the inadequacies they see in themselves.

Disrepair around the home equates with emotional despair. Broken furniture, cracked tiles, and crumbling plaster suggest broken dreams or a sense of hopelessness—your life seems to be falling down around you. Doors and windows that stick indicate feelings of being stuck or trapped by circumstances. Systems that don't work properly may symbolize self-imposed limits or areas in your life that aren't functioning adequately.

## NEW CLUTTER, OLD CLUTTER

In my home, clutter tends to collect in my office. As a freelance writer and artist, I'm often working on a number of projects simultaneously, and my desk may hold several stacks of paperwork that pertain to various jobs in progress.

"New clutter" of this sort usually indicates that you may be trying to do too much, that you lack focus and direction, or that you are letting things distract you from your primary path or purpose. New clutter can also include clothing lying around, toys or sporting equipment scattered about—things you've used recently, but haven't bothered to put away. Cleaning up this clutter can help you to become more centered, focused, and effective.

"Old clutter" is all that outdated, unused stuff that tends to get stashed in the basement, attic, closets, and garage. Old files, physical or digital, fall into this category, too. Lots of old clutter suggests you fear letting go of things that no longer have purpose in your life, even though they may actually be holding you back. Perhaps you are living in the past, are letting old ideas or emotions govern your present behavior, or are too security-conscious.

I used to work with a woman who never threw out any of the paperwork from her old jobs. Her files were stuffed with old folders, plans, cost sheets, etc. Although she rationalized that she might need to refer to this information someday, in reality she rarely did. With so much old clutter filling her drawers, the message she projected was that she didn't have room for new jobs, and so she subconsciously undermined her success. Once she realized the connection, she tossed most of her old paperwork and quickly attracted new business.

# WORKPLACE CLUTTER

Do stacks of papers, books, and file folders fill your work space? Do you have to shuffle through piles of paperwork to find something? On your computer, is your desktop a mess of icons? On your phone or tablet, are there apps you never use? Is your email inbox overflowing?

Disorganization in your work space wastes valuable time and money every day. How much does it cost you to search for misplaced or inaccessible materials, return phone calls because you can't put your finger on information when you need it, redo work, replace supplies that you stashed someplace but can't remember where, and so on? A carpenter I know has so much clutter in his truck and workshop that often he can't find a tool he needs and has to buy a duplicate. In some work environments, clutter can even lead to accidents and injury.

But clutter in your office has another drawback, too. It prevents you from focusing completely on the task at hand—your subconscious keeps reminding you of the unfinished business all around you. Over time, this can cause you to feel ineffective, unproductive, and overwhelmed.

## ACTIVITY CLUTTER

Multitasking has become a way of life in our modern world. We pride ourselves on being able to juggle a number of operations simultaneously. We check social media, talk to our loved ones, watch TV, go over our to-do lists, and eat breakfast all at the same time. At work, we follow the same pattern—scrolling through our email while talking on the phone, filing paperwork, and jotting down appointments on our calendars. Even when we're engaged in a single activity—particularly a mindless one like unloading the dishwasher or raking leaves—we're usually thinking about something other than the task at hand. Yet no matter how busy we are, we rarely feel a sense of accomplishment at the end of the day—most likely because we haven't truly experienced anything we've done.

When you try to do several things at once, you can't pay attention to—or enjoy—any of them fully. Confusion, stress, and forgetfulness are the inevitable results of this "activity clutter." How often have you put something down when you were involved in some other activity and forgotten where you left it? How many times do you have to ask someone to repeat what he or she just said because you were thinking about something else?

Narrowly focusing our attention and living in the moment reduces the confusion and stress produced by activity clutter. His Holiness the Dalai Lama even recommends against talking while you are eating, because in order to get the full benefit of either activity you must focus on it completely. When our attention is fragmented, we feel disconnected and derive less satisfaction from what we're doing. We end up missing out on what's going on right now—which is most of life!

Activity clutter also includes packing our days and nights with so many engagements, projects, and tasks that we rarely have a free moment to just be. One of the reasons we fill our lives with busyness is so we won't have to confront our feelings—and ourselves. To avoid looking deeply at ourselves, we scroll through social media, watch shows or movies, text or talk on the phone, do household chores, work out, go shopping.

Some of us load ourselves up with activities in order to boost our sense of importance. When many demands are placed on us, we feel needed. We don't delegate responsibilities to others because we like to think we're the only ones who can handle the job. If we're constantly doing something, we feel like we're making progress, even if we're really just spinning our wheels.

Controlling activity clutter requires you to examine your life and assign value to the various activities in which you engage. It may help to list out all the activities you participate in on a weekly basis. Put these activities under headings such as *Essential* (eating, going to work, doing laundry, etc.), *Enjoyable* (going to lunch with friends, playing the piano, reading bedtime stories to the children), *Optional* (shopping, watching TV, checking social media), and *Obligatory* (serving on a committee you wish you hadn't volunteered for, catering to an elderly relative's whims).

Examine your list with a critical eye, with the goal of reducing activity clutter by, say, 20 percent. Ask yourself some pointed questions: Are you devoting entirely too much time to some of the things on your list or doing them to avoid another part of life? For example, do you really need to watch every basketball game, pro and college? Are you letting someone else dictate how you spend your time or shouldering more than your fair share? Can you cut back on some of these duties, entrust them to someone else, or eliminate them entirely? What would happen if you did?

## RELATIONSHIP CLUTTER

Most of us know people we'd rather not spend time with, yet out of a sense of duty or guilt or good manners, we allow ourselves to be drawn into unwanted associations. Some of these people simply waste our time or distract us from more important things in our lives. Others actually drain our energy or have a negative influence on us.

There's no law that says you have to give time and energy to people you don't like or who aren't good for you. You don't have to be rude, but be clear and honest with these people. Depending on the circumstances, let them know you'd prefer not to spend as much time with them as you have in the past or that you don't wish to continue your association with them at all.

Even people we care about can clutter our lives with their problems, needs, and expectations. Family members, in particular, may not understand or respect the importance of personal boundaries. Friends may enjoy your company and want to include you in all their activities or share everything that's going on in their lives with you. If your friends or loved ones are cluttering your emotional space so that you feel you don't have enough time or energy for other things you want to do, set limits—for yourself and them. Learn to say no and stick to it. Explain, nicely, that you have work to do, need some time to yourself, are being drawn off-center—whatever the case may be. In relationships with other people, quality is more important than quantity.

Relationship clutter has another aspect, too. The *I Ching*, or *Book of Changes*, to which feng shui is closely connected, is not just an oracle, it's a three-thousand-year-old guide to living in harmony with the Universe. Much of the advice the *I Ching* offers involves relating to other people. Following its wisdom can help us eliminate clutter—confusion, tension, conflict, and other difficulties—in our personal relationships.

According to the *I Ching*, we clutter our relationships when we place too many of our own expectations on other people—when we expect them to fulfill our desires or satisfy our demands. A father who expects his son to be the star athlete he always wanted to be in his own youth, for example, adds clutter to the son's life. The need for ego gratification can also produce relationship clutter. If, for instance, we constantly look to other people to validate us or to boost our egos, we make unreasonable demands on them and may take offense if they don't give us the attention we want. In chapter 8, I include some tips for reducing this sort of relationship clutter.

## MENTAL CLUTTER

Memory gaps are more often due to inattention and "mental clutter" than to actual disease or intellectual decline. The truth is, most of us, regardless of age, lack mental focus and clarity—our minds constantly swirl with thoughts. We've become an attention deficit disorder society.

To see just how cluttered your mind is, set a timer for one minute. Try to hold a single thought for that brief span of time—it's harder than you might imagine. How many other thoughts popped into your head?

Mental clutter keeps us from being as productive as we could be. We derail our trains of thought thousands of times a day. Each time we allow ourselves to become sidetracked, we lose momentum.

Smartphones and TV are two of the most common and insidious sources of mental clutter. Our phones are always by our sides, pinging us with notifications and tempting us to check our email or newsfeeds even when we just looked at them two minutes ago. Streaming services have made it easier than ever to watch one thing after another, sometimes without processing what we've seen. Many of us leave the set turned on as background noise, where it continues to clutter the subconscious mind. Much of what we see onscreen is not just useless information, it's damaging to our mental clarity and peace of mind. Your mind retains everything it witnesses and stores it someplace in your brain, even if you aren't aware that this is happening. Do you really need to watch multiple news clips about the same story, morning, noon, and night? Repeated viewing of scenes of violence, tragedy, political conflict, and so on can be mentally and emotionally disconcerting. Studies have shown that people who consume a lot of mass media believe the world is a more dangerous place than those who rarely do.

Meditation is one of the best ways to reduce mental clutter. Meditating for just ten minutes each day will improve your concentration and clarity, calm nervous tension and stress, and increase your sense of well-being. Some people who meditate regularly say it produces all sorts of other benefits, too, such as helping them to sleep better, enriching their creativity, diminishing worries and fears, and enhancing their relationships with others. Professional athletes have even improved their skills as a result of daily meditation.

# ATMOSPHERIC CLUTTER

Have you ever walked into a room and felt bad vibes, even though you couldn't identify the cause? Buildings retain the energetic vibrations of their inhabitants for a long time—especially vibrations generated by strong emotions. The combined vibes produced by all the feelings, actions, sounds, and even thoughts of the people who have spent time in your home can add up to atmospheric clutter.

Therefore, it's a good idea to "clear the air" in your home periodically. Open the windows and allow fresh air to circulate through your space. *Smudging* is an easy and pleasant way to cleanse your environment of atmospheric clutter. White sage is one of the best materials for smudging, but incense—particularly pine, peppermint, eucalyptus, or sandalwood—will work fine, too. Light a bundle, cone, or stick of sage or incense and let its fragrant smoke waft through each room of your home.

Perform this purifying ritual to disperse unwanted vibrations before you move into a new place. You'll also want to cleanse your home after an argument or other distressing experience, after a party or large gathering, or when you sense that the space feels uncomfortable in any way. Furniture, jewelry, and other objects also retain the vibrations of previous owners, so before you use them, smudge antiques and preowned items to remove traces of other people's energy.

CH

3

# CLEAR YOUR CLUTTER,
# CLEAR YOUR LIFE

"**A**ll items produce sound, smell, color, texture, or shape and have various energies that can clutter and block optimum function. Having too many items can dilute the special energies of items that you love and that are purposeful in their placement," explains feng shui consultant Jami Lin. "The less clutter you have, the more your favorite items can be featured and radiate their life-enhancing energies."

This doesn't mean you should pare down your belongings until your home is as bare-bones as a Zen monastery. I have a friend who prides himself on his clutter-free existence. By rejecting possessions, however, he reveals his reluctance to place value on anything or to make commitments to people, community, and personal goals. The objects with which we surround ourselves—particularly those we prize most—say a lot about us. The point is to highlight your treasures—the things that give you joy to use, wear, or look at, regardless of their monetary worth—and eliminate those that have no particular significance. Getting rid of clutter is like weeding a garden so the flowers have room to thrive.

What to save and what to toss is an entirely personal matter. The renowned English designer and craftsman William Morris believed you should "have nothing in your houses that you do not know to be useful or believe to be beautiful." The same idea is at the heart of Marie Kondo and *The Life-Changing Magic of Tidying Up*: don't keep anything that doesn't "spark joy." That's good advice to follow when you are trying to decide what stays and what goes. If you still can't make up your mind, box items you aren't ready to part with yet, label the boxes, and store them for a period of time, maybe six months to a year. At a later date, you can reconsider how important they are to you.

## THE BAGUA

The Chinese believe that all life is interconnected, that our environments influence us and we influence our environments. To a feng shui master, your home presents a detailed and revealing picture of you—it shows which parts of your life are in good working order and which ones could use a little TLC.

Some popular types of feng shui employ an octagon-shaped tool called the *bagua* (pronounced *bah-kwah*) to determine which parts of your home correspond to which areas of your life. This device has links to the *I Ching*, but you don't need to plumb the depths of ancient Chinese wisdom to use the bagua. All you have to do is lay it over a sketch or floor plan of your home. See diagram on the following page.

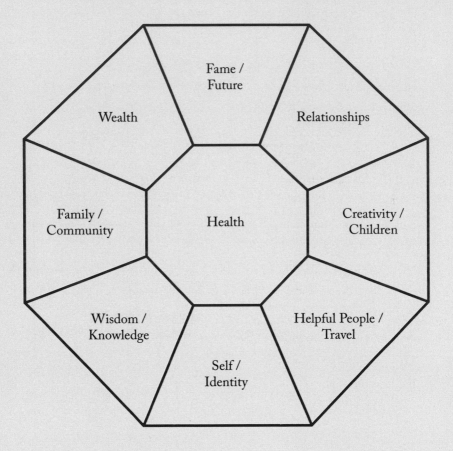

As you can see in this diagram, the bagua is divided into nine sectors, called *gua*, each one relating to a different facet of your life:

- **Health:** Physical well-being or challenges

- **Fame/Future:** Your public image, how you project yourself in the world, your career, future goals, and potential

- **Relationships:** Marriage or romantic partner(s), your attitudes toward love and relationships, interactions with a partner(s)

- **Creativity/Children:** Children of the mind or body, self-expression, creative endeavors

- **Helpful People/Travel:** Friends, associates, support network (including doctors, attorneys, accountants, mechanics, etc.), travel

- **Self/Identity:** Your self-image, your sense of identity, your work or purpose in life

- **Wisdom/Knowledge:** Your attitudes toward knowledge, your spiritual path, how you learn and share information

- **Family/Community:** Your parents, extended family, heritage, neighbors, and community

- **Wealth:** Your finances, your ability to earn, attract, and hold on to money

# USING THE BAGUA

The entrance you use most often to go in and out of your home is the starting point for analyzing your living space with the bagua. This may be a side or backdoor, or even an entryway through a garage, rather than the front door. If you live in an apartment building, the door to your own apartment is more important to consider than the main entrance to the building.

Align the arrow on the bagua at the center of the wall in which this door is placed, so that the octagon is superimposed on your home's interior. You can do this in your mind's eye, or physically lay a bagua over a drawing of your home's floor plan. Your entrance will fall in the Self Gua, Wisdom Gua, or Helpful People Gua.

Some schools of feng shui say you should use the front door as your reference point, even if you generally enter through the backdoor, but I haven't found this practice to produce accurate results. You may want to try both methods and decide for yourself which one works best.

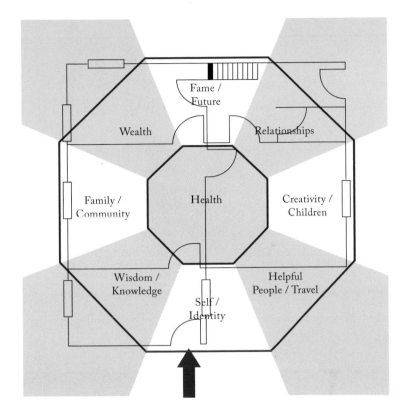

Now you can see which gua correspond to which rooms or areas of your home. Once you've identified the different gua in your home, you can quickly see which parts of your life are being adversely affected by clutter and set about clearing them.

I once visited the home of a couple of Texas artisans who wanted to know how they could improve their finances. Most of the time they entered and left their home via the garage. When I mentally positioned the bagua over their floor plan, their Wealth Gua turned out to be almost completely occupied by two very large closets that were jammed full of stuff. I suggested that they immediately start using their front door instead, which would rearrange the order of the gua in their home. I also recommended getting rid of some of the clutter in their closets in order to make room for new moneymaking possibilities to enter their life. A week after they started using their front door, the woman won $1,500 in a contest and the couple sold $5,000 worth of their artwork. The next week, the man (who is also a realtor) sold a half-million-dollar house he'd had listed for more than two years. You can bet they're believers now!

You can also analyze each room of your home using the bagua in the same way. Position the bagua so that the arrow lines up with the entrance to the room (or the wall in which this entrance is placed). The different gua will align with the various parts of the room. In this way, you can fine-tune your home and the related parts of your life.

For instance, you may notice that although your living room is generally pretty neat, the section that corresponds to neighbors is cluttered. This might show that even though your social life is relatively happy, you are experiencing some problems with your immediate neighbors. Clearing the clutter in this portion of the room can enable you to clarify the situation outside your home.

The bagua can also give you a bigger picture if you superimpose it over a plot plan of your yard (or, if you live in an apartment, over the entire building). Line up the arrow with the entrance to the property—your driveway, for instance, or the main entrance to an apartment building. The back left portion of your yard is the Wealth Gua, the back right section is the Relationships Gua, and so on. Like the interior of your home, your yard graphically describes what's going on in your life.

Shortly after I got divorced, a tree in my yard that had died during the previous year (while my marriage was deteriorating) fell down in a big storm. Interestingly, the tree was located just about where the Relationships Gua and the Creativity Gua intersect. The dead tree obviously symbolized the end of my marriage, but its collapse turned out to be a positive symbol: My former husband had not been very supportive of my creative endeavors, and when the dead tree toppled over, it indicated that the divorce had cleared the way for me to spend more time writing and painting.

As this example shows, the condition of your yard also impacts your life. Keeping your property clutter-free and well maintained has a positive effect on your health, wealth, and happiness. In Part Two, I offer a number of feng shui cures that you can do outside your home to increase the benefits you attract.

## WHAT DOES YOUR HOME SAY ABOUT YOU?

If you're like most people, some areas of your home are more orderly than others—like my friend who only cluttered up his Relationships Gua. A cluttered Family Gua, for instance, suggests confusion, stress, or disharmony among family members. A messy Wealth Gua usually indicates that your finances are unsettled, chaotic, troublesome, or that you aren't comfortable handling money matters. A Wealth Gua that's jam-packed with stuff, like the one in the home of the Texas couple, shows that profitable opportunities are blocked and/or your income is stagnant.

A friend who admits to being the world's worst housekeeper has a particularly unsightly Wealth Gua in her home. This bright and talented woman is always struggling to make ends meet. She comes from a family that overemphasized wealth and used money as a tool for manipulation. Not surprisingly, she has some issues concerning money and is unconsciously undermining her financial success by cluttering up her home. Although she often talks about cleaning and organizing her messy house, she never seems to get around to it—and probably won't, until she decides to address her confusion over money, values, and self-worth.

In the process of clearing the clutter in your own environment, you may find that you encounter some emotional resistance. Even though you haven't worn that coat or used that waffle iron in years, you may be reluctant to let go of it. Ask yourself why you are holding on to something—the answers could be quite revealing.

What's so fascinating about feng shui is that once you recognize that you are creating your own life situations with your attitudes—and that these attitudes are mirrored in the physical condition of your home—you can rectify the problems. By controlling clutter, you can literally take control of your life.

As you begin clearing the clutter from the various gua, you'll notice changes starting to take place in your life. Often these changes occur over a period of time, but sometimes they happen almost immediately. The day my "significant other" started tearing down walls and ripping up carpet in the master bedroom of a house he'd purchased for our winter home in another part of the country, I began feeling agitated—even though I was two thousand miles away and thought the project wouldn't get underway until the following week. I felt disoriented and disrupted—just like the physical changes that were taking place in the master bedroom. Walls were coming down, new windows and doors and closets were going in, and so on. You may be amazed at how even a few, simple adjustments can affect your finances or love life. For this reason, you may not want to tackle everything at once. Instead, choose one gua—or a portion of a gua—and put that in order. Wait a while and see what changes come about before cleaning up another section.

# MISSING GUA

Unless your home is a perfect square, rectangle, circle, or octagon, you may be missing part of or a whole gua. Usually this means that a portion of your life is absent, problematic, or unimportant to you. Don't despair—feng shui provides cures for just about every irregularity, including missing gua.

If you are a homeowner and can physically remedy this deficiency, you may want to build a deck, patio, garden, or other addition to complete the missing sector. If that's not an option, you can fill in the gap with what's called a "symbolic corner." Using your imagination, extend the footprint of your home to a point where the missing walls would join. Place something here to mark the symbolic corner—a plant, light, flagpole, statue, birdbath, large stone, etc.

If you live in an apartment and can't make major changes in the building's structure, you can symbolically cut holes in the walls that chop up your living space and eliminate a gua. Simply hang mirrors on the walls that cut off the gua to symbolically expand your apartment beyond its physical limitations. Or, if you prefer, hang pictures of landscapes with distant views to create the illusion of space beyond the actual walls of your apartment.

# SYMBOLIC ASSOCIATIONS

As we've already seen, much of feng shui relies on symbols and symbolic associations. In the process of uncluttering your home, consider the associations you attach to the things you choose to keep. Function, monetary worth, and sentimental value are only part of the picture. Even if an area is clutter-free, the symbolism of the articles you place there can have tremendous impact. Think about the meaning of a particular gua and whether the items you plan to put in it are compatible with the gua's significance—and your own intentions.

Here's a story that perfectly illustrates what I mean. A divorced woman I know wanted to find new love, but her relationships never seemed to go beyond an initial date or two. When I examined the Relationships Gua of her bedroom, I discovered the reason. On top of a chest of drawers in this section, she'd placed a jewelry box, and inside the box were pieces of jewelry her former husband had given her—including her old engagement and wedding rings! These items had monetary value and she didn't want to part with them, but the symbolic connections kept her bound to her ex and prevented her from attracting a new partner. Soon after she moved the jewelry to a safe-deposit box, the woman began a new relationship.

● Mirrors can be used inside to symbollically "cut through" obstructing walls.

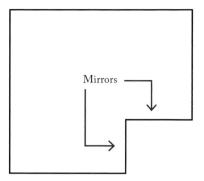

● Lights used outside can "fill in" missing sectors of an L-shaped building. A tree could produce the same effect.

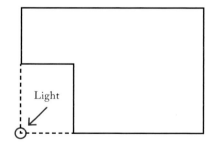

You can intentionally use symbols for specific purposes or to produce desired results. Coins, crowns, gems, champagne, and pictures of castles or Cadillacs, for instance, are symbols we associate with wealth. When placed in the Wealth Gua of your home or workplace, they encourage prosperity. We connect hearts, flowers, and doves with love, so these symbols can have a beneficial influence when placed in your Relationships Gua. Although some symbols mean pretty much the same thing to everyone, others are personal and may hold special significance for you alone. One spring, for example, a bird built a nest in a wreath I'd hung on my front door; soon three baby birds appeared. I took this as a positive indicator of creativity and new opportunities coming my way—and indeed, I soon received a contract to write a new book.

Shapes are simple symbols, too. Circles, for example, are universal symbols of wholeness and union. Arrows point in a certain direction and suggest movement. In feng shui, we can tap the deeper meanings inherent in shapes to create the circumstances we desire. Often, feng shui cures (including some of those in Part Two) use shapes to produce effects. The following list briefly explains the meanings of some familiar geometric shapes.

# SHAPES AND THEIR MEANINGS

**circle** = wholeness, continuity, unity, harmony, heaven

**square** = solidity, permanence, stability, earth

**triangle** = movement, change, direction toward a goal

**rectangle** = growth, expansion

**curved or wavy lines** = flexibility, interaction, adaptability

**straight lines** = rapid movement, single-mindedness

Although we tend to think of numbers as tools for counting and quantifying, they also have symbolic associations. Two, for instance, represents partnership. As you go about reducing clutter in your living and work spaces, keep in mind the number of items you choose to leave or highlight in a certain gua and the significance attached to them. If you hope to attract a mate, you don't want to clear away all but one object in your Relationships Gua!

Chinese tradition considers the number three and its multiples—especially nine—to be lucky. The following list explains the feng shui symbolism generally connected with numbers.

**1** = individuality, beginnings, focus

**2** = partnership, polarity, balance

**3** = expansion, creativity, action, opportunity

**4** = stability, solidity, form

**5** = change, movement, instability

**6** = harmony, supportiveness, give-and-take

**7** = introspection, solitude, wisdom

**8** = permanence, business, money

**9** = completion, fullness, good fortune

Even the materials used in your home or office furnishings have symbolic associations in feng shui. According to the Chinese Wu Xing philosophy, the world is composed of five elements—fire, earth, water, wood, and metal. Each of these elements depicts a different aspect of ch'i and operates in its own unique way to produce a specific effect. Fire stimulates, earth stabilizes, water softens and blends, wood expands, metal strengthens and concentrates.

As you go about reducing clutter and creating order in your life, you'll want to take into account the elemental balance in your living and work environments to prevent "elemental clutter." Too much fire in a room can cause tension and instability; too much metal can result in rigidity. In much the same way that you might prepare a recipe, you can combine and adjust the elements in your home or workplace in any way you choose to bring about the conditions you desire. For example, add metal objects to children's bedrooms to help them concentrate and focus on their studies. Add wooden items to your office to encourage new business and financial growth.

You don't have to be a feng shui master to incorporate the five elements auspiciously in your home or workplace—the following table shows which everyday objects fall into which elemental category. (Some actually incorporate two elements—a brick fireplace, for instance, blends fire and earth.) Your goal is to combine the elements in your environment so that all are represented and no single element overwhelms the others.

# THE FIVE ELEMENTS

| FIRE | EARTH | WATER | WOOD | METAL |
|------|-------|-------|------|-------|
| electricity | brick | glass items | wooden items | pots and pans |
| candles | stone | sink | paper items | silverware |
| fireplace | ceramic | toilet | plants | refrigerator |
| stove | tile | tub | linens | hand tools |
| lighting | marble | pool | books | other metal items |
| computer | porcelain | plumbing | newspapers | |
| heating system | rugs | aquarium | | |
| TV/sound system | | washing machine | | |
| clothes dryer | | windows | | |
| | | dishwasher | | |

# CLUTTER IN THE WORKPLACE

Many of us spend almost as much time at work as we do at home. Therefore, it's important to use feng shui in your place of employment, too. In China, huge multinational companies as well as tiny noodle shops employ feng shui practitioners to help them optimize their business prospects.

The building in which a company is housed describes the condition of the business itself. Have you ever noticed how some locations never seem to be able to support a business for very long and the occupant turnover rate is quite rapid? From a feng shui perspective, it's usually easy to see why.

You can use the bagua to analyze your workplace, just as you did your home. Simply superimpose the octagon over a floor plan or diagram of the store, office building, factory, or wherever you work to see which gua relate to which sections of the operation.

Workplace clutter can increase stress, interfere with clear communication, cause delays and mistakes, disrupt plans, and result in general confusion that can impair the prosperity, success, and well-being of all concerned. In some workplaces, such as restaurant kitchens and factories where potentially dangerous equipment is used, clutter can even lead to injuries.

In a work environment, clutter has a detrimental effect on each individual in the organization as well as on the overall company. Most of us have experienced problems associated with clutter in our workplaces. Perhaps you've wasted time hunting through stacks of file folders that weren't put away properly, or missed a meeting because the email announcing it was buried in your inbox. As companies cut back on their workforces to save money and employees are required to handle ever-increasing workloads, clutter-free environments become even more essential to the smooth operation of business. In chapter 5, I offer some quick and easy tips for improving your work environment by clearing physical and atmospheric clutter.

The various gua describe situations similar to those they relate to in a home. The Helpful People Gua, for example, represents suppliers, distributors, colleagues, bankers, lawyers, advisors, etc.; the Relationships Gua symbolizes professional contacts and interactions between workers. Obviously, the Wealth Gua and Fame/Future Gua are very important, and careful attention should be paid to these areas. If your business uses a cash drawer or safe, put it in the Wealth Gua. If travel is a major part of your business, keep this area in top-notch condition.

Some years ago, I worked for a firm that was housed in a beautifully renovated schoolhouse. The offices were conveniently laid out, with high ceilings, lots of windows, and attractive color schemes. The lobby was handsomely furnished with antiques. However, a large, practically empty conference room occupied the Wealth Gua. The room was rarely used—in fact, one of its primary purposes seemed to be for storage of boxes of stuff that nobody knew what to do with. Shortly after I left the company, it ran into financial trouble, and before long most of the employees had been laid off. I often wonder what might have happened had that important section of the building been better utilized.

PART
TWO

# Tips for Organizing Your House

CH

4

# CONTROL CLUTTER
# IN YOUR HOME

**Make sure the entrance to your home is clear and accessible.**
Visitors to your home get their first impressions of you from your entrance. Make certain your front door, porch, steps, and other nearby areas are neat, so they speak well of you. Ch'i comes in through the doors of your home, too. A cluttered or obstructed entrance blocks this life-generating force and inhibits your health, wealth, and happiness.

**Keep your entryway clear of clutter.**
The entryway or foyer serves as a transition zone from the outside to the interior of your home. To make guests—and ch'i—feel welcome, this area should be neat, clear, and inviting. Obstacles in this space that make it difficult for visitors to move into the other parts of your home will also interfere with the amount of ch'i that can enter and energize your life.

## Hang a wind chime in your entryway.

To prevent ch'i from getting stuck in your entryway, hang a wind chime from the ceiling. The chime symbolically circulates positive energy throughout your home. Its pleasing sound also breaks up atmospheric clutter that can collect in a small, windowless, or self-contained foyer, mudroom, or anteroom. Ring the chime upon entering to clear the air.

## Clear the walkways through your home.

Keep the pathways through your home free of furniture, clutter, and other obstructions. Can you move comfortably from one room to the next? Can you easily access windows and closets? Or do you have to sidestep walls, furnishings, or piles of clutter? Obstacles in your home's passageways block the smooth flow of ch'i into the various gua and limit the benefits it brings.

## Dust lampshades.

Lamps symbolize the sun's life-giving energy and promote positive feelings. From the perspective of feng shui, light boosts your vitality, stimulates opportunity, and encourages growth. Keep lampshades clean to maximize the amount of light in your home. Additionally, be sure to turn on the lights periodically in rooms or areas that don't get used often—this keeps ch'i from stagnating in these spots.

### Clean out a closet in your living room.

Closets symbolize the hidden parts of ourselves. When you clean out and neatly organize a closet, you demonstrate your willingness to remove old attitudes, habits, and behavior patterns that can cause confusion or blockages in your life. Because the living room is the place where socializing often takes place, cleaning out a closet here, if you have one, can improve your social life. This cure also can have a positive effect on your public image and your interactions with other people in general.

### Clean out a closet in your Wealth Gua.

If a closet in your Wealth Gua is jam-packed with stuff, you may be blocking new moneymaking opportunities. To make room for prosperity to enter your life, clean out a closet in your Wealth Gua. Getting rid of clutter here can also help you uncover hidden issues you may be harboring about money and what it represents to you.

### Clean out a closet in your Relationships Gua.

Many of us have old attitudes, fears, and "baggage" that can cause problems in our romantic relationships. Just closing the door on problems won't make them go away. By cleaning out a closet in your Relationships Gua, you demonstrate your willingness to address these issues. If your goal is to attract new love into your life, you'll increase your chances if you first let go of old stuff that keeps you stuck in the past. Getting rid of clutter can also improve an existing relationship by eliminating obstacles, resentments, rigidity, and confusion.

**Keep closet doors shut.**

Closets represent the private side of your life, because this is where you store things out of sight when you aren't using them. Even after you've uncluttered your closets, keep their doors shut to prevent personal matters from becoming public knowledge.

**Install clothing rods at various heights.**

Garments hang at different lengths, so positioning clothing rods at varying heights increases the usable space in your closet. Instead of running a single rod the full length of a closet, install one full-width rod high up and another below it that runs only partway across. You can use the partial-height section to hold shorter items—shirts, jackets, vests, and skirts—and the full-height area for dresses, slacks, coats, and longer garments.

**Use the one-a-day clutter-clearing method.**

If clearing away your clutter seems like an overwhelming task, take it a step at a time. Just get rid of one thing you don't need each day— throw it out, give it to someone else who'll enjoy it, recycle it, or donate it to charity.

**Choose a personal color palette and only buy clothing in that palette.**

Most people look better in some colors than in others. Determine what your best colors are and only buy clothing in those hues. This allows you to reduce the number of garments in your closet while actually increasing your wardrobe's versatility, because everything goes with everything else. This cure also facilitates shopping—you can bypass everything that isn't in your personal color palette.

**Get rid of clothing that doesn't go with anything else.**

Do you have garments that don't coordinate with anything else in your closet? Usually this means that either the color or the style isn't really you. Pass them on to someone who'll appreciate them.

**Eliminate duplicates.**

How many white shirts, black skirts, or blue striped ties do you really need? Pare down your wardrobe by eliminating duplicate items. Keep the ones you like best and that look best on you—perhaps two per season. Take the rest to a consignment shop or donate them to charity.

**Pack away off-season clothes as soon as you stop wearing them.**
From a practical point of view, this uncluttering cure frees up closet and drawer space and makes it easier to find what you want to wear. On a psychological level, it enables you to put the past behind you so you can move forward and embrace each new season of your life.

**Get rid of clothing you no longer wear.**
If you haven't worn something in a year, you probably don't need it. Unless a garment has special significance, it doesn't warrant space in your closet or dresser. Give it to a friend or charity—or take it to a consignment shop where your clutter can earn cash.

**Don't hold on to clothes that don't fit.**
If you're trying to lose or gain weight, you may undermine your success by holding on to clothes that are a larger or smaller size than your target. Additionally, keeping clothes that are the wrong size can make you feel bad about yourself even if you look and feel great. Get rid of garments that don't fit your current self—even if they might fit you again down the road, your style might have changed by then.

## *Arrange your wardrobe.*

There are many ways to organize your wardrobe. Choose the one that best suits your needs.

### Group similar items together.

Hang clothing so that similar items are grouped together and you won't have to search through your entire closet to locate a particular garment. Designate drawers for specific items—place garments you wear on the upper part of your body in the top drawers, and put jeans, shorts, etc., in the lower drawers.

### Group clothing by color.

This saves time by enabling you to see at a glance what goes with what. Odd items that don't match anything else will immediately stand out—get rid of these.

### Organize clothing according to frequency of use.

In your closet and dresser drawers, place items you wear frequently where you can access them conveniently. Hang or store "special occasion" garments in less accessible areas. If you always wear particular items together, hang them together.

**Buy underwear once a year.**

Underwear tends to get bedraggled after a year or so. Replace it all in one shopping trip to save time, then throw out old undies. If you color coordinate bras and panties, this practice allows you to match up items—colors may change from season to season. (A friend of mine throws out all her old underwear when a relationship ends and treats herself to new lingerie as a way of symbolically inviting new love into her life.)

**Mend holes in pockets.**

Literally as well as symbolically, holes in the pockets of clothing allow money to slip away. Mend them!

**Reduce suitcase clutter.**

If you're going on a trip, lay out all the clothing you plan to take with you on your bed. Then, put half of it back in your closet and pack what's left. (Choosing clothing within a limited color range makes this easier and increases the versatility of the outfits you pack.) If possible, try to fit everything you need for a short trip into a carry-on bag—you won't have to pay extra fees, wait for your luggage when you arrive, or risk losing it en route.

**Store suitcases inside one another.**

Suitcases take up a lot of room. Store smaller suitcases inside larger ones when you pack them away—many luggage sets come sized this way intentionally. You can also store other items, such as off-season clothing or items you only use for travel, inside suitcases if your space is limited.

**Don't iron clothing before packing it.**

This saves time and effort, as garments tend to get crumpled in your suitcase regardless of how carefully you pack them. Wait until you get where you're going to iron clothes rather than doing it twice.

**Remove odd socks from your dresser drawer.**

Socks that have been separated from their mates for several weeks or more are probably destined to remain solo. Once a sock has lost its partner, remove it from your drawer. See page 78 for an extra tip about single socks.

**Label shoe boxes.**

If you store your shoes in boxes to protect them, eliminate guesswork by labeling the boxes so you can see at a glance what's inside. Clear, stackable plastic boxes with lids that allow you to see your shoes work great, too.

**Organize shoes to reduce closet clutter.**

Even if you don't have a huge collection, shoes can still clutter up your closet. Group them according to season, color, style, and frequency of use. Keep shoes you wear regularly in the most convenient place. Store special-occasion shoes farther back. If space is limited, move off-season shoes out of your primary clothes closet. Here again, the "how many do you really need" rule applies—if you have six pairs of black heels, you can probably get rid of a couple of pairs.

**Use plastic bags to stuff the toes of shoes.**

Most of us have more plastic bags than we know what to do with. Instead of using expensive wooden shoe trees to keep your shoes in shape, stuff the toes of your shoes with wadded-up plastic bags.

**Get rid of broken jewelry and pieces you don't wear.**
Gemstones retain energetic vibrations for a long time—that's why some psychics can "read" a person from their jewelry. Repair or get rid of broken jewelry, which can signify breaks in your relationships, your career path, or your finances. Either give pieces you don't wear to someone who will enjoy them or take them to a consignment shop.

**Organize jewelry conveniently.**
Bait and tackle boxes, like the ones fishermen use, are great for organizing jewelry. The small compartments keep earrings together and prevent necklaces from getting tangled. Fasten the clasps on necklaces when you aren't wearing them to prevent tangles.

**Keep jewelry neat while traveling.**
When you're traveling, use plastic organizers designed for pills and vitamins to keep earrings and other jewelry neat. Some stores and vitamin companies offer these handy containers free with purchases.

**Wash your mirrors.**
In feng shui, mirrors are very powerful cures because they visually "double" what they reflect. A dirty mirror obstructs and diminishes this power. Keep mirrors clean and sparkling—and pay attention to the views they reflect.

**Neatly arrange objects in front of a mirror.**

Because of the doubling effect mirrors have, it's extra important to neatly arrange any objects you place in front of a mirror. If a mirror is reflecting clutter, it will exacerbate confusion, chaos, problems, or upsets.

**Place treasures in front of a mirror.**

Just as mirrors can amplify the negative effects of clutter, they can also amplify the positive effects of objects that hold special meaning for you or that symbolize things you want to expand in your life. To increase your prosperity, for instance, set one of your personal treasures or an item that you associate with wealth where it will be reflected in a mirror. To further enhance the power of this cure, place the mirror and the object in the appropriate gua in your home—see chapter 3 for information about the different gua and their associations.

**Turn single socks into dust cloths.**

You don't have to toss odd socks—recycle them into dust cloths. Slip a soft cotton sock onto your hand and use it to wipe down shelves, tabletops, and other furniture. They also make great cleaning cloths for mirrors and windows. As you clean, remember that windows and mirrors are symbolically linked with vision—washing them can help you to more clearly see a situation in your life.

**Dust bedroom furniture.**

Has your love life lost its luster? Dust bedroom furniture and give it a coat of oil or polish. This cure symbolically revitalizes your love life and helps to make it sparkle again. Think loving thoughts while you perform this cure.

**Furnish bedrooms with even-numbered items.**
Odd numbers are associated with change, movement, and activity.
If you place three or five pieces of furniture in a bedroom, you may
generate restless energy that can disrupt sleep.

**Furnish your home with beds of the same size.**
If possible, use the same size bed in each bedroom—all full or queen
size, for instance. You won't have to purchase and store sheets in
several different sizes, and you can easily interchange bedding as
necessary. Buying linens in neutral colors or a single color palette will
increase their versatility and allow you to reduce the number of sheets,
blankets, etc., that you need.

**Wash sheets and put them straight back on the bed.**
On laundry day, take the sheets off your bed and wash them. Instead of
making the bed with a different set and folding and storing the freshly
washed set, put the same sheets (now clean) back on your bed. On
cold nights, making your bed with warm sheets fresh from the dryer is
especially nice!

### Don't store stuff under your bed.

Clutter under your bed blocks the smooth flow of ch'i and may disrupt sleep. Blocked ch'i can also produce confusion, obstacles, or stagnant conditions between you and a partner with whom you share the bed. If your living space is limited and you must utilize the area under your bed, be sure to neatly organize what you stash there. Pay attention to the symbolism attached to the items you place beneath your bed, too. Sharp objects, for instance, may produce subconscious feelings of discomfort that could disturb your sleep.

### Vacuum under your bed.

Dirt and dust can aggravate allergies or other health problems and interfere with restful sleep. From the perspective of feng shui, dust acts as a magnet for stuck ch'i, which can lead to irritability, diminished vitality, and other complaints.

### Don't let your bedroom become a dumping ground.

If you allow all sorts of stuff to collect in your bedroom—ostensibly because you don't have anyplace else to put it—you create clutter that can cause distraction and confusion in a romantic relationship. Assess whether the articles you store in your bedroom are appropriate to the room's purpose. If not, find another location for them or consider getting rid of them.

### Don't let clutter accumulate on your nightstand.

Clutter on your nightstand can produce confusion in your love life, because the bedroom is a private zone devoted to intimate activities. Bedroom clutter can also generate stress that may disturb your sleep—particularly when the clutter is near your head. You spend one-third of your life sleeping, so it's especially important to keep your bedroom clutter-free.

**Place a small bell on your nightstand or dresser and ring it each time you enter your bedroom.**

This simple ritual clears the air of unwanted vibrations that could interfere with your sleep. A bell can also act as a trigger and send a signal to your subconscious that it's time to relax. It can focus your attention on intimate matters, too, and may help you attract love into your life.

**Keep screens out of your bedroom.**

A TV or computer brings influences from the outside world into your private space. This mental clutter can interfere with your love life or adversely affect your ability to sleep peacefully—especially if you watch the news or an upsetting or violent show before retiring. Even if you watch something peaceful, the blue light these screens emit disrupts your body's production of melatonin, which prepares your body for sleep. If you live in a studio apartment and don't have anywhere else to put them, cover your screens at night to minimize their influence. Use a standalone alarm clock so you can keep your smartphone out of the bedroom, too, or at least avoid scrolling through the news or social media in bed.

**Don't let dirty laundry collect in your bedroom.**

Dirty laundry holds on to stale energy, which can have an adverse influence on your health and vitality. Don't let it mount up in your bedroom, where it can interfere with your well-being.

### Reduce the number of objects in a small room.

In a small room, quantity is even more important than size. Clutter really becomes apparent when space is limited, so limit the number of furnishings and accessories when decorating a small room. This allows the eye to focus on what's really important instead of jumping around from item to item, which can be distracting and confusing.

### Use larger pieces of furniture in a small room.

At first, this seems to go against logic. But if you place only a few small pieces of furniture in a small room (having already eliminated unnecessary furnishings and accessories), your room will either seem spartan or like a dollhouse. Larger objects give a small room a sense of drama, purpose, and stability.

### Reposition furniture that obstructs access.

A piece of furniture that blocks traffic into or through a room is an inconvenience to you and others—it also obstructs the smooth flow of ch'i. Move pieces that jut into pathways, interfere with opening doors, etc. If necessary, reduce the number of items in the room.

### Rearrange furniture periodically.

To keep your life from becoming static, rearrange furnishings from time to time. One of the fundamental principles of feng shui is that when you make changes in your home, you spark changes in your life, too. Rearrange furniture in your bedroom to perk up your love life; move furniture in your living room to stimulate friendships. To keep changes manageable, move furniture around in one room or area at a time—too much change all at once can be unsettling.

### Sketch a room to scale before buying furniture.

Measure your room and sketch it to scale before purchasing new furnishings. Note the locations of windows, doorways, stairs, heating and air-conditioning elements, and so on. You may think you know what will fit, but pieces don't look the same in a large showroom as they will in your home. Take the sketch with you when you go furniture shopping so you'll know if that terrific sofa or antique armoire will work in your space—you'll save time and money.

### Keep your gua in mind when you buy new furnishings.

When you purchase new furniture, think about which gua it will occupy. Are the shape, color, function, and symbolism of the item compatible with the gua's meaning—and your intentions? For instance, if you are redecorating a room in the Relationships Gua, you might want to include a pair of lamps, chairs, or nightstands instead of just one. Objects with curved lines encourage harmony when placed in the Family Gua, whereas sharp angles and straight lines tend to stimulate individual activity and tension.

### Use a consistent color scheme throughout your home.

Decorating each room with a different color scheme produces "color clutter" that can be psychologically jarring. If you use a consistent color scheme with only slight variations or accents of different hues, you'll create a sense of harmony throughout your home. This decorating trick also gives you greater versatility—you can move pieces from one room to another without the colors clashing.

**Limit the number of colors in each room.**

Although monochromatic decorating schemes can be boring,
combining too many different hues and patterns in a room may also
produce color clutter. Limit your palette to three colors to create
a sense of harmony. If you decide to include a variety of patterned
objects in the same room, make sure they all contain the same colors
so they seem related. Vary the size and type of the patterns you use
together—small florals and broad stripes, for instance—so they don't
compete with one another for your attention.

### Smudge your home.

Smudging gets rid of bad vibes in your home that may be interfering with your health, wealth, or happiness. Clear the air by burning bundled sage, or sage incense, to purify the space and remove emotional clutter. This is especially important when you move into a new home or after an argument.

### Smudge antiques and other used objects to purify them.

Objects that have been owned by someone else can retain the vibrations of other people and places. Therefore, it's a good idea to cleanse antiques and other used items before letting them take up residence in your home. Use the smoke from burning incense or dried sage to smudge and purify preowned articles.

### Open all the windows in your home periodically.

This clears the air and disperses stagnant energy along with atmospheric clutter that can build up in a closed space.

### Wash your windows.

In feng shui, windows symbolize the eyes. Clean windows allow you to see a situation clearly. If you are experiencing confusion in a particular area of your life, wash the windows in the part of your home that corresponds to that area. (See chapter 3 for more information about the different gua and their associations.)

**Sweep cobwebs from the corners of your home.**
Cobwebs symbolize the past—sweep them away to remove stuck energy, attitudes, and emotions.

**Clean your window screens.**
Dirty screens cut down on the amount of light that comes through your windows. Ch'i enters your home via the windows, too, but dust-clogged screens prevent this life-giving force from reaching the interior. To maximize the light your home receives, it's important not only to wash the windows but to keep screens clean as well.

**Use salt to remove bad vibes.**
Sprinkle a pinch of salt in the corners of your home to clear away disruptive or unwanted energies. Salt also protects your home from ambient bad vibes.

### Alphabetize spices.

Many herbs and spices come in nearly identical jars or tins, or you may have a permanent set of containers you reuse. Alphabetical organization enables you to find what you need quickly and prevents you from grabbing the wrong one by mistake. Before you replace spices, assess your needs with a critical eye—it may not be space- or cost-effective to buy something you'll only use once a year.

### Discard old spices.

Spices lose their potency over time. Throw out any that have been sitting around for too long.

### Contain condiments.

Use a tray with handles to hold condiments you use regularly. This keeps them neat in your fridge or on a counter and makes it easy to carry all of them to the table together.

### Clean out your refrigerator.

Not only is spoiled food smelly and unhealthy, it clutters up your refrigerator. Cleaning out your refrigerator on a weekly basis makes it easier to find things, cuts down on waste, and prevents bacteria from building up. Rework leftovers into soups, stews, or casseroles.

### Organize your refrigerator.

After you've disposed of old food, organize the contents of your refrigerator efficiently. Arrange similar products (such as lunch meats) or items you are likely to use together (like salad fixings) next to each other. Position perishable foods, such as fruits and vegetables, in the front of your refrigerator. Tall containers can be placed farther back, but keep small items where they are clearly visible so they don't get lost behind larger products. Place a paper towel or silicone mat under anything that might drip or spill, to minimize cleanup later.

### Wipe off containers.

Wipe off salad dressing bottles, condiments, juice containers, and other potentially messy items before you put them back in the refrigerator or cabinet.

### Clean your stove.

Feng shui practitioners believe that the stove generates wealth. Keep yours clean and in good working order to encourage prosperity. To keep the stream of prosperity flowing in your direction, turn on your stove's burners briefly each day, even if you don't actually cook anything.

### Hang pots and pans.

Pots and pans are easily accessible when hung from an overhead rack, wall hooks, or a pegboard—especially in kitchens with limited cabinet space.

### Store nonstick pans safely.

To keep nonstick (Teflon) surfaces from getting scratched, place a towel or silicone pad between pots and pans when you stack them in a cabinet, closet, or drawer.

### Store large pans inside your oven.

If storage space is limited in your kitchen, store large iron skillets, cookie trays, etc., inside your oven when it's not being used.

### Hang cooking utensils above the stove.

Keep cooking utensils handy and neat by hanging them on hooks, a rack, or a magnetic strip above your stove or cooktop. If your stove is in an island, an overhead hanging rack provides a convenient place for storing cooking equipment.

### Organize kitchen utensils and equipment according to their frequency of use.

View kitchen counters, drawers, and cabinets as high-priced real estate, and only store items there if you use them regularly. Place utensils and other equipment close to where they will be used—cooking items near the stove, cleaning products under the sink, preparation tools in cabinets and drawers at the prep counter, and so on.

### Clear kitchen countertops of clutter.

According to feng shui, the kitchen is connected with prosperity. By keeping your countertops neat and orderly, you can reduce money-related stress and confusion. From a practical point of view, of course, uncluttered countertops allow you to work more efficiently. Place only the things you use every day on your kitchen countertops.

## Store items you rarely use away from your kitchen's primary work area.

Don't let highly specialized appliances and seasonal items clutter up your kitchen. For example, rather than keeping pasta makers, fondue pots, and punch bowls in your kitchen cabinets, store them in a hall closet or another less accessible area.

## Evaluate small appliances.

Small specialty appliances, such as bread makers, pressure cookers, and espresso makers, should be subjected to the same rigid standards as clothing—if you haven't used it in a year or more, ask yourself if you really need it. Many of these rarely used items take up more than their fair share of room in your kitchen. Consider passing them on to someone who'll use them more often.

**Wipe up spills immediately.**

Spills are inevitable on stoves and in refrigerators. Wipe them up immediately, before they harden or burn into a formidable mess.

**Use hanging baskets for kitchen gadgets.**

Especially handy in a small kitchen, hanging baskets offer a convenient and attractive way to store gadgets such as corkscrews, bottle openers, potato peelers, wooden spoons, serving tools, etc.

**Choose reusable coffee filters.**

Gold and stainless-steel coffee filters eliminate the need for paper ones and are available in basket, cone, and disc styles to suit whichever way you brew your beans. A single filter lasts a long time, cutting down on your daily waste, and because these metals don't interact with the coffee, your morning beverage actually tastes better.

**Stack plates and napkins together.**

To keep china plates from being scratched or chipped, stack them with a folded cloth napkin between each plate. This not only prevents damage, it facilitates setting the table because you grab both plates and napkins at the same time.

**Clear clutter from your dining room table.**

If you don't use your dining room table very often, it may end up being a clutter collector. Clutter on your dining room table can produce tension or problems between members of your household—clear it away promptly.

**Clean out the space under your kitchen sink.**

Throw out old cleaning products that may have lost their effectiveness and move potentially harmful ones to a place where young children won't be able to reach them. To reduce clutter under your sink, buy cleaning products that have multiple uses.

**Organize cleaning materials in a basket with a handle.**

Organize assorted cleaning materials for floors, tile, windows, porcelain, and so on in a basket with a handle and store it under your kitchen sink. When you clean bathrooms, carry the basket with you—that way, you won't have to keep duplicate collections of cleaning products in different rooms.

**Store recycling bins out of sight.**

Like the contents of wastebaskets, recyclables symbolize things that have served their purpose and are now destined to leave your life. Put the bins in a spot where their clutter will not attract your attention and remind you of the past.

**Empty wastebaskets.**

Trash signifies old, cast-off stuff you no longer want or need. Pay attention to where you position wastebaskets by using the bagua, as discussed in chapter 3. Empty them daily to prevent stuck ch'i from building up in your home.

**Divvy up cleaning chores with a partner or roommate.**
One person may hate to vacuum but not mind cleaning the bathroom.
Another might enjoy cooking but not like to wash dishes. Divide tasks with
a partner or roommate according to individual preferences, so that each
assumes a fair share of the housekeeping burden.

**Put things away as soon as you've finished using them.**
Rather than letting stuff pile up, get in the habit of putting away clothes,
books, games, etc., as soon as you've finished using them.

**When you pick something up, do something with it.**
Don't just relocate a magazine, your slippers, or a dish to another temporary
spot—put it where it belongs. Wash a dirty glass or file paperwork right
away so you don't have to come back to it later on. Once you get in the
habit of doing this, you'll find you don't waste as much time looking for
things, either.

## Vacuum heating ducts and elements.

Like fireplaces and woodstoves, heating systems are connected with vitality and growth. From the perspective of feng shui, vacuuming dust from heating ducts, vents, etc., allows more positive energy to circulate through your home. From a practical point of view, this cure will make your system function more efficiently and cut down on heating bills.

## Clean your fireplace or woodstove.

A dirty fireplace or woodstove is both inefficient and unsafe. In feng shui, the fire element is linked with growth, vigor, enterprise, and creativity. On a symbolic level, therefore, an ash-filled fireplace or stove can limit your vitality, enthusiasm, and good luck. Keep them clean and in good operation.

### Install a ceiling fan.

This cure stirs up sluggish ch'i while dispersing atmospheric clutter, hot air, stuffiness, and unpleasant aromas in your home. Ceiling fans can also reduce heating and air-conditioning bills.

### Keep tools handy.

Collect basic, essential tools—a hammer and nails, screwdrivers, pliers, etc.—in a wire basket and keep it in a convenient place. If you don't have to search for the right tool, you're more likely to take care of minor repair jobs promptly.

**Fix something that has been annoying you.**

From a practical perspective, this cure alleviates a condition that is a source of irritation to you—a clock that doesn't keep accurate time, a drawer that doesn't close properly, a cracked piece of tile. Symbolically, you are demonstrating your willingness to correct areas of your life that aren't as good as they could be.

**Utilize closet doors for storage.**

Affix narrow shelves, racks, grids, hooks, or pegboards on the inside of closet doors to maximize storage space. (Remember to keep closet doors shut.)

**Make the most of vertical space.**

Especially in small apartments where floor space and closets are at a premium, utilize the space at the top of a room. Expand your home's storage space with baskets, shelves, and racks hung above the fridge, chests of drawers, file cabinets, toilet, and so on.

**Get rid of old paint cans.**

After you paint a room or area of your home, it may be a good idea to keep a small amount of paint for touch-ups. Over time, however, your walls will change color slightly due to sunlight, age, smoke, and other factors, so the paint in the can will no longer match. It also tends to dry up or separate, rendering it unusable. Storing old paint might not be wise from a health perspective either, as some paints, varnishes, and finishes contain toxic substances. Cans of paint take up a lot of room, too—don't bother saving them for more than a year.

**Clean out your basement.**

The basement symbolizes your subconscious. By cleaning out your basement, you address past conditions or repressed issues that may have been lingering in your subconscious. If this uncluttering task seems overwhelming, break it down into manageable components. For example, clean only a corner or section of your basement at a time.

**Clean out your attic.**

The attic represents your mind and spiritual path. Cleaning up clutter in the attic makes room for new ideas and promotes mental clarity. This task, like cleaning your basement, can be broken down into small segments and accomplished over a period of time so it doesn't seem so intimidating.

### Have a yard sale.

Turn clutter into cash by holding a yard sale. This cure accomplishes two prosperity goals—making money and getting rid of clutter—simultaneously. To encourage family togetherness or neighborhood unity, hold a group sale—it's more fun, too.

### Get rid of objects that have unpleasant associations for you.

Items that remind you of unpleasant experiences or people you don't like can be a subtle source of annoyance. Instead of letting them trigger negative thoughts and feelings, get rid of them.

### Get rid of gifts you don't like or never use.

Just because you received something as a wedding present or housewarming gift doesn't mean you have to hold on to it forever. If you don't like it or never use it, pass it on to someone who will.

### Discourage physical gifts from friends whose taste is different from yours.

Although friends and loved ones may mean well, sometimes their taste and yours just don't mesh. Instead of accepting gifts from them that you know you'll never use, ask them to donate money in your name to a favorite charity.

### Give consumable gifts to friends.

Rather than buying friends and family members more stuff, give them consumable presents—concert or theater tickets, gift certificates to a favorite restaurant, gourmet foods, fancy soaps, etc. Treat them to something special they might not get to enjoy otherwise.

### Return borrowed items.

Is other people's stuff cluttering up your home? Return things you've borrowed from friends and neighbors promptly so they don't pile up in your living space. Because objects retain their owners' energies, other people's belongings may bring distracting vibes into your home.

### Share rarely used items with friends.

How often do you use a punch bowl, picnic basket, or hedge trimmer? Consider sharing some of these rarely used items with friends or family members, rather than each of you purchasing your own. If it's convenient, you may wish to share the ownership and responsibility of larger items, too, such as vacuum cleaners or lawn mowers. This practice frees up storage space and saves everyone money.

### Share media with friends.

Although you may want to watch your favorite movies several times, you can reduce clutter in your entertainment area by sharing DVDs and Blu-rays with friends—especially those big box sets of entire shows. Create a library with close friends and family members rather than buying duplicate copies. Also, consider buying digital copies instead of discs to avoid taking up any physical space at all. That is, if you don't just stream everything.

**Use coat trees.**
Old-school standing coat trees can be a convenient and decorative way to keep hats and coats neat. If someone in the family suffers from closet phobia, put a coat tree in his or her bedroom. Use one in the bathroom to replace or supplement towel bars.

**Provide a place for keys.**
Instead of hunting for your keys, place hooks, a basket, or a bowl near your home's entrance to keep keys handy.

**Discard old keys.**
If you can't remember what a key fits and haven't used it in ages, get rid of it.

**Remove sharp objects from your Relationships Gua.**
Sharp or pointed objects can produce discomfort, cutting words, or harsh exchanges between you and a romantic partner. Don't place them in your Relationships Gua—move them to another spot to reduce arguments.

**Push chairs in when you're not using them.**
Get in the habit of pushing chairs back under your table or desk after you leave it. They not only look neater that way, they also don't jut out into passageways, where they can cause stubbed toes and interfere with the smooth flow of ch'i through your home.

**Group objects in your Family Gua to encourage family unity.**
Select an item to represent each member of the family and place these
in a prominent place in your Family Gua. Tie the objects together with a
pretty red ribbon to symbolize togetherness (red symbolizes good luck in
Chinese culture). Clear away from this area any items that suggest conflict,
competition, unhappiness, or disruption.

**Toss old love letters.**
Holding on to letters from old flames can keep new love from entering your
life. Discard reminders of past romances and you'll make room for new
possibilities to come your way.

**Throw out old postcards, invitations, date books, birthday cards,
and other mementos.**
Unless there's something truly precious about these markers from your past
or you're planning to write your memoir, you probably don't need to hold on
to them for the rest of your life. You'll still have your memories without the
paper trail. If you're having trouble of getting rid of certain items, you could
comprise by scanning or photographing them and tossing the originals.

**Save good photographs, dump bad ones.**
Sort through old photographs and eliminate those that aren't clear, flattering, informative, or special in some way. Dump pictures that don't favorably depict you and others, as well as any of people you don't remember or like.

**Organize photos.**
After weeding out the poor photographs, organize the keepers into albums or digital folders, preferably in chronological order or by subject.

**Remove photos of people other than you or your romantic partner from your bedroom.**
Pictures of other people—friends, family members, etc.—draw your attention to them and distract your energy away from your romantic partner. Unclutter your bedroom of these photos and the emotional energy attached to them.

### Frame favorite photos.

Select your absolute favorite photographs and frame them. "Gallery" frames that group a number of photos within a single frame keep memories alive and can be great conversation starters. Or, use your imagination to create a photo collage.

### Group pictures on walls.

Unclutter your walls by grouping paintings, photographs, etc., according to size, subject, style, or colors. Pictures in a variety of sizes and shapes can be hung in a pleasing arrangement that is itself a composition. Create a grid and sketch the configuration to scale on paper before you begin hammering nails into your walls.

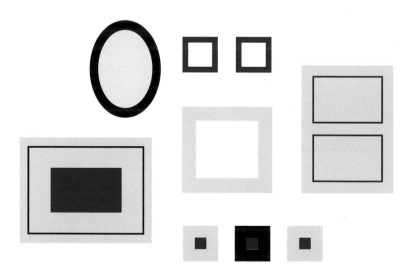

## Group decorative objects on a mantel, table, or shelf.

If you have many decorative objects you want to display, grouping them can prevent a cluttered appearance. Place similar items together. Because numbers have special meanings in feng shui, you may want to arrange objects in pairs to encourage cooperation, threes to stimulate action or change, or fours to promote stability. (See chapter 3 for more about number symbolism.)

## Rotate artwork periodically.

If you have lots of artwork and can't display it all at once without creating a cluttered effect, rotate your art. Museums do this regularly to keep their collections fresh and exciting. Rotating artwork in your home prevents ch'i from getting stuck, too. Changing the pictures on your walls can also help you get a new perspective on a situation.

## Hang artwork on a stairway wall.

Stairway walls tend to be underused as places to display artwork. Hanging pictures alongside stairs also attracts ch'i and encourages it to move up to the next story of your home, energizing your living environment on every level.

## Turn clutter into art.

Scraps of old lace, antique buttons, foreign postage stamps, photos, odd earrings, seashells, and other bits and pieces can be combined into attractive collages. Use your creativity to transform miscellaneous clutter into works of art—then frame them in shadow boxes and hang them on your walls (preferably in your Creativity Gua).

**Pay attention to objects that have special significance for you.**
Enjoy your favorite objects—don't just let them sit there, collecting dust.
When you use, admire, or otherwise appreciate your treasures, you invest
them with positive energy and activate the intentions associated with
them. Spotlight them in a place of honor in your home.

**Organize hobby items neatly in the Creativity Gua.**
Place painting supplies, quilting materials, beer-making equipment, and
so on together in baskets, bins, or a trunk and store them in the Creativity
Gua. This keeps hobby articles from spilling over into other parts of the
home while simultaneously sparking your creativity.

**Spark your creativity with threes.**
Neatly display three paintings, sculptures, or other works of art that
you particularly like in your Creativity Gua, in order to spark your
imagination. (Three is the number of creative activity and represents
giving form to ideas.)

**Store sports equipment on racks.**
Sporting goods can take up lots of space in your home. Use racks and
hooks to hang up tennis racquets, golf clubs, bicycles, helmets, skates,
etc., and keep them orderly. Don't hang on to tennis balls that have
lost their bounce, golf balls with dings, and so on. Each member of
the family should assume responsibility for hanging up his or her own
athletic equipment.

**Use a laundry basket to hold stuff for short trips.**

If you'll be traveling somewhere by car, toss odds and ends you want to take with you into a plastic laundry basket. You can carry the basket easily from room to room and from house to car. Last-minute items can be added without opening and repacking a suitcase.

**Take a laundry basket to the pool or beach.**

Lightweight and waterproof, plastic laundry baskets are great for holding beach or pool gear, too. Toys, towels, sunblock, sandals, snorkeling equipment, snacks, and so on stay neatly contained in the car en route and can be quickly packed up again when it's time to head home.

### Place four objects in your Wealth Gua.

Four is the number of permanence and security. If you have trouble holding on to money, choose four objects that symbolize wealth to you. Neatly arrange these in your Wealth Gua to help stabilize your financial situation.

### Collect loose change in a money jar.

Place a large, attractive jar in your Wealth Gua. Each time you drop a coin in the jar, concentrate on your intention to attract abundance. This practice lets you "prime the pump" and start prosperity flowing your way. When the jar is full, take them to the bank and trade them in for paper money. Then start filling up your money jar again.

### Organize receipts.

Use a box, expandable file, binder, or other convenient container for receipts. Organize receipts in clearly marked envelopes so you can find them easily. Arrange them by date, category, etc. Save receipts you'll need for tax purposes in one box, receipts for appliances or equipment with warranties in another, receipts for gifts or personal purchases you may have to return in another, and so on. If you keep receipts digitally, sort them into a series of folders or use an organizer app to get them sorted.

**Trim houseplants.**

Plants symbolize growth—keep yours neatly trimmed to encourage new growth in your life. Dry, brown leaves are not only unattractive, they represent death, decay, and stagnant conditions. Spindly vines suggest things are growing out of control and need to be reined in.

**Wash your plants' leaves.**

Living plants are a favorite feng shui cure—place a plant in an area where you want to encourage growth (see chapter 3 for information about the different gua and their associations). To help plants grow and look better, wash dust off their leaves periodically so they can breathe. Loosen compacted soil so air can circulate to their roots, too.

## Throw out wilted flowers.

Fresh flowers signify blossoming situations and, like live plants, they generate positive vibrations. But once they start to droop, throw them out—wilted blooms suggest decline and death. Flowers have long been associated with love, so place a vase of fresh flowers in your Relationships Gua to brighten your love life.

## Change the decoration on your front door each season.

This gesture keeps your entryway looking pretty and up-to-date. It also acknowledges the changes in nature—and life—and helps you stay in step with the times.

## Pare down holiday decorations.

Holiday decorations are used only for a short period of time and can take up more than their fair share of space during the rest of the year. Sort through these seasonal items and weed out the ones that you don't really like or that don't have special meaning for you. Those you choose to keep will escalate in sentimental value.

## Pack small, fragile items in coffee cans.

Protect fragile holiday decorations, such as Christmas tree ornaments, by wrapping them in tissue paper or bubble wrap and storing them in coffee cans. Label the cans so you know which ornaments are inside without having to unwrap them. Coffee cans are ideal for storing or shipping other breakables, too.

### Give away books you've finished reading.

Although you might want to reread classics and a few favorite novels periodically, most books can be passed on to friends or donated after you've finished reading them. Reference texts you use frequently, autographed books, and those that have special significance can stay.

### Organize books.

Whether you choose to group them by author, subject, or the Dewey decimal system, books should be organized on your shelves so they're easy to locate and look neat.

### Organize magazines, journals, and newspapers.

Get rid of outdated periodicals so they don't continue to pile up. Holding on to "old news" can block new ideas from emerging. Recycle newspapers and take magazines to hospitals, nursing homes, or coin-operated laundries for others to read.

### Organize your music.

Organize music by artist, genre, or another method to encourage easy access. Give away CDs you rarely listen to (or have copied to your computer), or trade them in at a used music shop. Store any physical media you're keeping in a convenient rack, drawer, or cabinet near your sound system. Prune your music collection annually—if you haven't listened to it in a year, you probably don't need it.

### Divide work, living, and rest areas.

In small apartments, one room may serve multiple purposes. Separate your sleeping area from your living and work areas with a decorative screen, curtain, or other divider. It's hard to relax fully and put daytime tasks aside if a cluttered desk is nearby, reminding you of all the things you still have to do.

### Establish a "temporary clutter" site.

Use a basket, plastic bin, box, or other container to temporarily hold clutter you can't deal with immediately. At least once a week, go through this container and organize or toss the contents to prevent a buildup of clutter.

### Update your contacts list.

Whether you keep track of phone numbers and emails on your phone or in a physical address book, this organizing cure works to improve your relationships with other people by causing you to focus on your connections with them and the roles they play in your life. Like all uncluttering cures, it also reduces confusion and saves time by making it easier for you to find addresses and phone numbers.

### Groom pets regularly.

Especially in warm weather, pets can shed copious amounts of hair. To keep fur residue from collecting in your home, groom pets regularly—outside, if possible. This practice has side benefits, too. Studies have shown that petting an animal companion can reduce stress, and it also strengthens the bond between you and your pet.

### Place maps and travel guides in your Travel Gua.

Maps, books and magazines about foreign places, pictures of far-off locales, globes, and other items that symbolize travel can open up opportunities for adventure if you organize them neatly in your Travel Gua.

### Keep cosmetics in order.

Keep cosmetics neat and orderly in trays, baskets, or containers with lots of small sections or dividers. Favorite items you use every day can stay in your medicine cabinet or in an attractive holder on your bathroom vanity. Move specialty products to another spot.

### Discard old cosmetics.

Do you have a dozen lipsticks but only use two or three favorite shades? Toss the rest to reduce clutter in your medicine cabinet. Old cosmetics can dry out, lose their effectiveness, or become breeding grounds for bacteria, too—if you haven't used it in six months (three for mascara or liquid eyeliner), dump it.

### Throw away old medications.

Outdated medications not only clutter your medicine cabinet, they may lose potency over time and become less effective. To reduce clutter and prevent potential health problems, throw away prescription and over-the-counter medications that have outlived their expiration dates. Follow disposal instructions on the medication's package, if there are any, and consult the FDA website if you're not sure of the right way to get rid of something.

**Create "product consensus" among family members.**
Although each member of your family may prefer—or need—certain
specialized personal care products, you might be able to agree on some
general-use items such as shampoo, soap, or toothpaste. Rather than
cluttering up your bathroom with lots of different products, try to reach a
consensus on as many items as possible.

**Evaluate bulk buying.**
Buying in bulk may not be that good a deal if you have to find room to
store large quantities of items you won't use in a relatively short period
of time. A better solution might be purchasing bulk products in common
with family members or friends, so everyone saves money without
incurring excess clutter.

**Buy light bulbs in one or two wattages.**
Rather than stocking up on an array of light bulbs in every wattage,
choose a couple of convenient options—maybe 60 and 100 watts—that
will serve most of your lighting needs.

**Buy only what you need.**
It can be tempting to buy something when it's on sale. But remember, a
good deal is only a deal if you really need it and are going to use it soon.

**Don't shop during the full moon.**
During this lunar phase, we tend to behave impulsively and are more
likely to buy things we don't really need. Unless you absolutely have to,
don't go shopping around the time of the full moon—and make sure
anything you buy on a whim can be returned.

CH

5

# CONTROL CLUTTER IN YOUR WORKPLACE

**Make sure the entrance to your office or place of business is easily accessible and free of obstacles.**

Your entrance gives visitors their first impression of you and your business—make it as neat and attractive as possible so it conveys a positive image. This is also where ch'i enters, bringing creative energy and prosperity with it. Clear any clutter, litter, or obstacles that could block the smooth flow of ch'i into your workplace. If your company is located in a building with many other offices, do what you can to improve the main entrance to the building as well as the entrance to your own business.

**Clean, polish, and maintain the sign for your place of business.**

Like the entrance to your business, your sign conveys an image of your company to prospective clients. If it is dirty or in disrepair, people will get the impression that your business isn't sound or that you don't care about your work. Make sure your company's sign is attractive so clients—and helpful ch'i—will be drawn to you.

**Clean up the sidewalk and street near your place of business.**

Litter and other clutter near your place of business creates an unsightly impression and can detract from your success. Don't just clean your entryway, take it a step further and tidy the surrounding areas, too.

**Keep your waiting room clean and orderly.**

The lobby or waiting room serves as a transition zone between the outside and inside of your workplace. Clients and customers develop their initial feelings about you and your business while sitting in your waiting room. Organize reading materials neatly, empty wastebaskets, dust tables, wash windows, and make sure furnishings are clean. (Clean restrooms are essential, too.)

**Smudge your lobby, foyer, and waiting room.**

Smudge public areas in your place of business each evening. This practice removes the vibrations left by former clients and keeps them from influencing others. The preferred way to do this is by burning sage or incense, but you can also clear the air with aromatherapy light rings or diffusers that release cleansing scents (such as mint or citrus) into the area. It's a good idea to periodically smudge conference rooms and individual offices or cubicles, too. By doing this right before you close up for the night, the smoke and scent will be gone in the morning before anyone with a sensitivity might arrive.

### Clear passageways through your work area.

When the paths through your work area are free of obstructions, you can move about easily in the space—and so can ch'i. An obstacle-free work space allows you to work more efficiently. Clear pathways also encourage prosperity because they allow ch'i to flow into all areas of the workplace, infusing them with life-giving energy.

### Superimpose the bagua over your workplace.

Place the eight-sided bagua over a blueprint or floor plan of your workplace, just as you did with the floor plan of your home. Align the arrow at the center of the wall that holds the entrance to your place of business (or your own office entrance). Now you can see which areas of your workplace correspond to which parts of your professional life. (See chapter 3 for a diagram of the bagua.)

### Replace burned-out light bulbs in your office or work area.

In feng shui, light symbolizes the sun and helps to stimulate positive energy and growth. Burned-out light bulbs diminish vitality and can cause finances and/or business opportunities to languish. Keep your financial picture bright by replacing light bulbs as soon as they burn out. In some cases, you may wish to replace a bulb with one of a higher wattage to increase the amount of energy being generated in a particular area.

### Dust, clean, and polish your point of sale.

If your place of business has a cash register, Square, or other point of sale device—including tablets and other portable card readers—make sure it's clean and sparkling. Dust, grime, chipped paint, and corrosion discourage positive ch'i and can hamper your cash flow. Tip: Put your cash register in the Wealth Gua of your business to stimulate prosperity. Tie a red ribbon on it and put three *I Ching* coins in your cash drawer for good luck.

### Encourage wise decisions with the number eight.

Eight is the number of pragmatism, business, and finance. Place eight objects in the Wealth Gua of your workplace to encourage the practical utilization of money and other resources. Make sure the items you choose signify your intentions.

### Answer email promptly.

Keep email from cluttering up your inbox. If you respond to email as soon as you receive it, you'll keep your mind uncluttered, too.

### Delete emails regularly, rather than storing them.

Cleaning out old email is the electronic equivalent of eliminating old magazines, newspapers, and paper clutter. Delete messages as soon as you respond to them. If you want to save messages, create a special file for old email, and prune it regularly.

### Update your contacts list.

Do you have piles of business cards stuffed in your wallet? Are names and phone numbers scrawled on slips of paper? Update your contacts list regularly so you can find names, addresses, and phone numbers easily and do away with paper clutter. You'll also reduce the risk of losing someone's address or number.

**Answer snail mail promptly.**

Don't allow envelopes to pile up—they not only clutter your desk, they also serve as nagging reminders of unfinished business. Rather than wasting time rereading mail and memos, deal with them promptly. When you open a letter or bill, reply to it and then file it or throw it away.

**Return phone calls, texts, and other messages.**

Like the previous cures, this one clears up lingering obligations and gets them out of your way so you can stop thinking about them and move ahead. Returning messages promptly also demonstrates good manners and respect for the person contacting you.

**Remove old files from your computer or cloud storage.**
Pruning files you no longer need makes it easier to find what you want.
It also frees up space and, if you're deleting items from your hard drive,
speeds your computer's operation.

**Group digital files into as few top-level folders as possible.**
Set up a few subject categories and organize documents into subcategories
within the main subject groups. This makes it easier to find documents
and keeps your desktop neat.

**Back up your computer regularly.**
It's amazing how many people overlook this simple task. If your computer
fails (or is stolen), you won't have to waste valuable time redoing lost work
if you've backed up your files recently. At the end of each day, or when
you finish working on a particular project or document, back it up on an
external hard drive, flash drive, or cloud storage. If using physical media,
keep a backup copy of important work in a place outside your office—at
home, in a safe-deposit box, or in another location.

**Color-code appointments on your calendar.**
Design a system of colors to prioritize your appointments, such as red
for essential or ASAP, blue for less important or ongoing projects. This
method lets you see at a glance what you need to take care of first and
helps you to organize your time more effectively.

## Make your calendar fully reflect reality.

It may not be enough to just put an appointment on your calendar. To see at a glance how much time you really have available in a day, block out the whole amount of time each commitment actually takes up—for example, not just the length of an offsite meeting but the travel time to and from the location. This practice helps you keep from overbooking.

## Take care of sticky notes.

These constant reminders of things you haven't taken care of yet can distract you from the task at hand. Lots of little notes stuck all over your office can also make you feel inefficient or overwhelmed by unfinished business. Tend to them quickly, rather than letting them clutter up your office—you'll improve your productivity and your sense of accomplishment as a result.

### Remedy a missing gua in your office.

If your office or work space is irregularly shaped and has a notched-out section or a missing gua, you may be missing out on moneymaking opportunities. Hang mirrors on the walls of the missing corner to cut symbolic windows in these walls (see chapter 3 for more information). This cure opens up your space so your prosperity isn't limited.

### In an open office plan, group desks so everyone is comfortable.

Ideally, everyone should be seated so that he or she can clearly see the entrance to the room. This prevents workers from being startled or distracted by someone walking up behind them. In an open office situation that includes many desks, the ideal arrangement may not be possible. If some individuals must be seated with their back to the door, position mirrors so they can see the reflection of the entrance without having to turn around.

### Adjust doors in your work area so they open and close easily.

Doors that don't work properly impede the flow of ch'i through your workplace and can limit your prosperity. The door of your main entrance and doors in your Wealth Gua are the most crucial, but ill-fitting doors in any area can cause obstacles. Plane the edges of doors that stick, oil hinges, fix wobbly knobs, and so on so that everything operates easily.

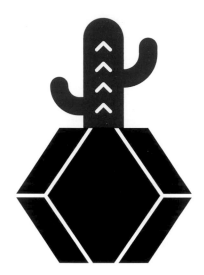

**Use plants to absorb emotional and mental clutter.**

When many people must work together in tight quarters, place plants between desks to provide a sense of privacy. Plants also absorb the energies emitted by many workers, reducing stress. In feng shui, plants are a favorite cure because they symbolize growth—encourage growth in your business by including a number of live plants in your office decor. (Remember to keep plants neatly trimmed and healthy—dead leaves signal decay and decline.)

### Get rid of metal objects to encourage flexibility.

The element of metal is associated with structure and rigidity. If you want to encourage spontaneity, change, and flexibility in your business—or the people who work there—reduce the number of metal items in the work area. Replace metal desks with wooden ones, for instance, to stimulate growth and new opportunities.

### Limit wooden objects to control growth.

Usually growth in a business is desirable, but growth that occurs too rapidly may be stressful or problematic. To control the rate of growth and create stability, move some wooden items out of the Self and Future Guas of your workplace. Replace them with metal ones, which symbolize structure. If, at a later date, you want to spark growth again, you can put the wooden pieces back. Experiment until you get the right mix to produce balance.

### Use an area rug to unite furniture.

To reduce the cluttered appearance of many pieces of furniture—especially in a small office or waiting room—place an area rug so that each piece of furniture rests partly on the rug. This decorating cure has an added advantage, too. By establishing visual unity, it symbolically brings together the different elements in the room and promotes workplace harmony. Consult the list of shapes and their meanings in chapter 3 to pick the type of rug that best aligns with your goals: A round or oval rug encourages cooperation, a rectangular one promotes growth, a square one increases stability.

**Place only items you use regularly on your desktop.**
Think of the top of your desk as the most valuable piece of real estate in your office. Only those things that you use in your daily routine, such as your computer, phone, and notepad, should be allotted this precious desktop space.

**Superimpose the bagua on your desktop.**
You can superimpose the octagon-shaped bagua over your desktop, just as you did with a floor plan of your workplace. This enables you to see which portion of your desk relates to which sector of the bagua. When you are seated at your desk, the far right-hand section describes your business relationships. The far left-hand part corresponds to money, the area to your near right signifies travel as well as people who can help you, and so on. Use this method to organize your desk and your work life. (Refer to the diagram of the bagua in chapter 3.)

**Use the eastern section of your desk for new business.**
The east, where the sun rises, is considered the point of new beginnings, so this can be a good spot to keep files and other materials that relate to new projects. Go through this paperwork daily to stay current. Move "in progress" materials to a different area. This keeps clutter from accumulating and makes room for new opportunities to continue flowing into your life.

**Clean off your desk at the end of each day.**
This practice lets you put your tasks "to bed" at the end of the workday. It also gives you a chance to catch anything that might have been misplaced or accidentally shoved under a pile of paperwork. In the morning, a clean desk invites you to start fresh, without feeling overwhelmed by tasks left over from yesterday.

**Rearrange objects on your desk periodically.**
This cure stirs up new possibilities and prevents your work situation and finances from growing stagnant. It also gives you a chance to reevaluate items—which ones do you really need and which are less important and can be moved off your desktop? In the process, you might even find something you thought was lost forever!

**Hang bins or baskets in your office.**

Hang baskets or wood, metal, or plastic bins on the walls in your office to reduce desktop clutter and keep paperwork handy.

**Organize small office supplies in a convenient desk drawer.**

Rather than letting tape, sticky notes, a stapler, paper clips, etc., clutter your desktop, move them to an easily accessible desk drawer. Keep loose items in an organizing tray, basket, or other sectioned holder to prevent them from shifting around in the drawer.

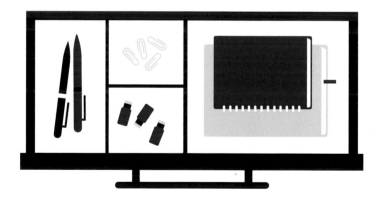

**Organize cosmetics in a pencil holder.**
Small cosmetics, such as lipstick, eyebrow pencils, and mascara, stay neatly organized in the compartments of a pencil holder—either a tray designed to attach inside a desk drawer or a portable case.

**Organize books, magazines, and other reading materials.**
Arrange books, trade magazines, and other reading or reference materials in a logical, convenient manner—by subject, title, date, author, or whatever method works best for you.

**Discard outdated reference materials.**
Recycle or discard old magazines and reference materials that you no longer use. Old literature not only creates clutter, it also can keep you stuck in the past and interfere with the flow of new ideas and information.

**Place reading materials in the Wisdom/Knowledge Gua.**
Organize books, magazines, trade journals, reference texts, and other reading materials in the Knowledge Gua of your office to stimulate the flow of information and ideas.

### Clean off a shelf in the top of a closet.

A cluttered overhead shelf in a closet suggests that you have problems hanging over your head. This condition can lead to stress or headaches—something might even fall from the shelf and hit you on the head! Get rid of things you aren't using and neatly organize the rest.

### Organize your supply closet.

Organize office supplies and arrange them according to use—group computer supplies together, mailing materials together, etc. Get rid of supplies you won't be using anymore when you update your office equipment or switch to other products. Place items you use often in easily accessible spots.

### Clear your Future Gua to encourage new business.

The number one represents new beginnings. To stimulate new opportunities, remove all but one significant item from the Future Gua of your work space. Make sure the object you choose to leave there has positive associations and is compatible, from a symbolic standpoint, with your goals, business, or future plans.

### Don't store old stuff in your Future Gua.

A storage closet or file cabinet full of old business can stifle growth and block new opportunities if it's in the Fame/Future Gua of your workplace. Clutter in this area can also cause other people to have a distorted or confused image of your business. Clear away anything that doesn't point to the future and encourage positive associations.

**Rearrange items on a table or shelf in your Wealth Gua.**

If your company's finances are sluggish, rearrange the objects on a shelf, table, or other piece of furniture in the Wealth Gua of the president or CEO's office (or the office of another principal). Whenever you make a change like this in a section of your workplace, you spark change in the corresponding area of your business. This cure helps get your cash flow moving again.

**Attract financial help from someone else.**

Six is the number of shared resources. To attract financial help from a partner, investor, bank, or other source, clear away all but six items from the Wealth Gua of your work space. The symbolic quality of these objects is important, too, so pay attention to the meanings attached to those that remain—they should have positive, prosperous associations for you. One of them could be a light or a live plant, as both cures encourage growth.

**Arrange ceramic items in your Wealth Gua to stabilize finances.**
If money seems to go out as fast as it comes in, neatly arrange objects
made of a ceramic material—tile, pottery, brick, stone—in the Wealth
Gua of your workplace. To make this cure even more effective and
improve money management at the same time, place four ceramic objects
in your Wealth Gua and hang a mirror behind them.

**Don't place a wastebasket in your Wealth Gua.**
You may end up "throwing away" your money on things you don't need or
unprofitable ventures if you put a wastebasket in the Wealth Gua of your
office. Move it!

**Keep wastebaskets hidden or in unobtrusive spots.**
Trash represents things you don't want or need. To prevent workers from
paying too much attention to things that are no longer useful, place
wastebaskets where they aren't obtrusive.

### Clean out your work bag or briefcase.

This cure is similar to cleaning out your desk or file cabinet, but it can be even more important for people whose work requires them to travel or conduct business outside of the office. Remove clutter to make room for new business and moneymaking opportunities. Get rid of old paperwork, names and addresses of people you no longer contact—anything you don't use or need.

### Throw away pens that don't write.

How many times have you grabbed a pen to jot down a message only to discover that it's out of ink or clogged? Instead of putting it back where it will annoy you again, throw it away.

### Use pencils with retractable lead.

Pencils with retractable lead never need to be sharpened, so they don't produce messy shavings. Whether you prefer disposable ones or distinctive refillable mechanical pencils, they are cleaner and more convenient than ordinary wooden pencils.

### Use a whiteboard for daily reminders.

Rather than posting lots of little notes around your office, use a dry-erase board instead. This keeps paper clutter to a minimum and encourages you to respond to messages promptly. A whiteboard also cuts down on waste and saves trees. Use different-colored markers to prioritize messages.

### Record your ideas with a notepad app.

Many people get bright ideas when they're walking, driving, waiting in line, or performing mindless, routine tasks. While most smart phones come with a note app, there are plenty of other useful, user-friendly ones that might fit your needs better. If you record brainstorms and inspirations, they won't get lost in the clutter of your daily work demands.

### Use a bullet journal for "bright ideas."

A bullet journal is a great way to keep track of to-do items and sudden strokes of genius in a single organized place—both your day-to-day and your distant future plans. You can find lots of instructions and advice for bullet journaling online, so do your research and go with the system that's right for you. The important thing is that you stick with your process and symbols so it's easy to use when you want to go back to something you wrote.

### Complete a task on your to-do list.

Unfinished tasks produce mental clutter and nag at you, making you feel ineffectual. Each time you complete a task, you experience a sense of satisfaction at having taken charge of your life and alleviated one more obstacle to your happiness. Whether it's a mental list, a daily sticky note, or a bullet journal, strive to check off as many items as possible each day.

### Color-code file folders.

When it comes to physical folders, using a color-coding system makes it easy to see at a glance what's in a crowded file drawer—it can also help you to spot outdated or misplaced files. Color-coding can be used in conjunction with other filing systems—alphabetical, chronological, etc.

### Put away files promptly, whether they're physical or digital.

How much time do you waste searching for files that weren't put away promptly or saved in the right place? As soon as you finish with a paper file, put it back so you and others can find it easily. (In an office where many people share common file cabinets or materials, this organizing task becomes even more imperative.) When someone emails you a file to keep for your records, save it immediately to the place where it needs to go—don't let it linger on your desktop or in your downloads folder.

### Work on one project at a time.

Don't try to juggle several projects simultaneously—it can be inefficient, confusing, and stressful. Focus on one thing at a time. It's best to keep files and materials related to other tasks stored away until you're ready to devote your attention to them. This also prevents paperwork from getting misfiled.

### Get rid of old files.

Cluttering up drawers with old files and paperwork, or letting old documents you no longer need sit on your computer or server, can block moneymaking opportunities. Remove outdated materials that may be keeping you stuck in the past to make room for new business to come your way.

### Follow through.

Allow enough time to finish a project once you start it. Follow through until you complete a task, or a designated portion of it. Each time you have to set work aside and come back to it, you clutter your mind with other thoughts and waste time refocusing your attention.

## Keep business meetings on track.

Create an agenda for meetings and stick to it. Don't allow discussions to wander off track. Rather than bringing in side issues that can clutter your focus and detract from the main points under consideration, schedule another meeting to deal with those concerns later.

## Place pairs of objects in the Relationships Gua.

This cure is especially valuable if you work in partnership with someone, but it can also improve interactions among coworkers. In the Relationships Gua of your workplace, arrange objects in pairs. Two is the number of cooperation, congeniality, and teamwork, so placing two chairs, two lamps, two pictures, etc., in this gua can have a positive effect on all business relationships.

## Eliminate sharp angles to improve communication.

Lots of straight lines and sharp angles in your workplace tend to increase single-mindedness and can interfere with give-and-take between coworkers. To improve communication and cooperation, remove objects with sharp corners or many angles.

## Remove sharp objects from the Relationships and Helpful People Guas of your office.

Scissors, letter openers, and other sharp objects placed in the Relationships Gua or the Helpful People Gua of your office can have a detrimental effect on your relationships with coworkers, colleagues, and clients. Sharp or pointed items symbolize cutting words, backstabbing, severed ties, and other hurtful conditions. Move these tools to another spot.

### Clean light fixture covers.

Dusty lampshades and light fixture covers cut down on the amount of light—and ch'i—flowing into your work space. Lights symbolize the sun, growth, clarity, and vitality. Increased light equates with a brighter financial picture and better overall well-being for your business.

### Wash the phone in your office.

From a practical standpoint, this helps to keep germs from spreading—especially if more than one person uses your office phone. Symbolically, washing your phone suggests that you are striving for clear communication with business associates and clients.

### Wash the windows in your office.

Ch'i enters a building through its windows. Clean windows let more light and positive energy into your work area, thereby improving your financial prospects and your firm's general well-being. Because windows represent a building's eyes in feng shui, clean windows allow you to see situations more clearly—symbolically as well as physically.

### Clean your computer screen.

This practical maintenance cure not only enables you to see your work more easily, it reinforces your intention to make the most of your income-producing capability. Dust on your computer screen can physically and symbolically interfere with your ability to clearly see the task before you. The more you use your computer, the more important this becomes—wipe down the screen frequently.

### Rein in cord clutter.

Some offices have systems for keeping electrical cords and computer cables hidden. In other cases, you can control them by tying them together neatly with twist ties or purpose-made cord wraps.

### Vacuum your office rug.

Vacuum or sweep your office floor at the end of each day. Then, when you enter your office in the morning, you'll symbolically step into a fresh environment full of opportunity. Because rugs and floors represent foundations, a floor that's free of dirt and clutter suggests an orderly, stable base under your feet.

**Hang a wind chime between your workplace and an obtrusive building.**

If you feel pressured by a neighboring building that's too close or much larger than yours, hang a wind chime between your office and the other building. The movement and pleasing sounds of the chimes disperse the disruptive atmospheric clutter and tension produced by the obtrusive structure and its occupants.

**Install fans to circulate positive ch'i.**

The windows of many large office buildings, warehouses, and other structures don't open to let fresh air circulate. As a result, ch'i can stagnate. Ceiling fans stir up stuck ch'i and disperse atmospheric clutter to reduce stress, stimulate new ideas, and promote healthy interaction between workers.

**Keep lunchrooms and break areas neat.**

These areas are intended as oases from the stress of the workplace, but if they are cluttered or dirty, they may have the opposite effect. Workers who can clear their minds periodically throughout the day tend to be more productive at their jobs. Messy break areas can also contribute to low morale, arguments, and general confusion, so keep these rooms neat, clean, and attractive.

**Ring a bell upon entering your office.**

The sound of the bell summons positive ch'i into your office and clears the air of unwanted vibes that can produce atmospheric clutter. This simple ritual can also serve as a trigger to stimulate your intention to get down to work and generate income. If you work in an office with other people, you might want to run this idea by them first to make sure they won't be annoyed with the sound. Maybe they'll even join in on the practice.

**Clear clutter from your Travel Gua.**

Clutter in your Travel Gua can cause confusion, delays, and mix-ups when traveling. To facilitate smooth and profitable business trips, make sure this sector in your workplace is neat and orderly. Organize materials related to travel—as well as those that your company uses in connection with shipping and receiving—in this gua.

### Create a focal point in your office or work space.

When your mind starts to wander, use a focal point to bring your attention back to your objective. Clutter distracts and scatters your attention; a focal point hones and directs it. Choose something attractive—a picture, a vase of flowers, a meaningful item—as your focal point. If your objective is to earn more money, place the focal point in the Wealth Gua of your workplace. If your reputation and public image are of primary importance, create a focal point in your Fame/Future Gua.

### Create a focal point in a waiting room.

Give clients and visitors something to focus on while they wait, to help keep their minds from wandering to other things. This focal point should be something that encourages positive feelings about your company and conveys beneficial energy. A large, healthy plant or floral arrangement, a tank full of colorful fish, attractive artwork, and handsomely framed inspirational sayings are a few possibilities.

### Use calming scents in your office or work area.

Soothing aromas, such as vanilla and lavender, can cut through mental clutter and help you stay calm under pressure. Depending on your office environment, you can burn incense, stash fragrant potpourri or a sachet in a drawer, or dab your wrists with essential oil to reduce stress and mental clutter. Be mindful of coworkers with scent sensitivities—their comfort comes first.

**Use stimulating scents to improve mental clarity.**

The refreshing scents of citrus and mint can help to keep you alert and increase mental clarity. Use these aromas in your personal space or (if your coworkers are onboard) diffuse them throughout your office environment to chase away sluggishness, stimulate the flow of new ideas, and improve communication between workers.

**Hire help when you need it.**

Although you may prefer to do everything yourself—or feel that you should—sometimes it pays to hire other people to help out. Overloading yourself with tasks can cause stress and burnout. It may not even be cost-effective if low-level functions are taking up time and energy you could be devoting to more important ones.

CH

6

# CONTROL CLUTTER
# OUTSIDE YOUR HOME

### Recycle.

Recycle everything you can. This eco-friendly practice reduces clutter in our world, to everyone's advantage.

### Buy recycled products.

Recycling waste is only half the solution to the ever-expanding buildup of garbage in our world. When you buy products made from recycled materials, you support efforts to decrease waste and encourage companies to seek environmentally friendly solutions.

### Clean up the sidewalk and street near your home.

Accumulated trash, dead leaves, and other debris make the area around your home unsightly and can interfere with the smooth flow of ch'i. Clear away this clutter to create a positive first impression of your home and community, and to improve relationships with neighbors.

### Fix cracked or broken pavement in a driveway or sidewalk.

Like many feng shui cures, this one has both a practical and a symbolic side. Repair a damaged sidewalk or driveway to encourage the smooth flow of ch'i to your home and to prevent accidents.

**Trim shrubs and trees near your home's entrance.**

Plants give off positive vibrations and are usually considered assets. But if they are overgrown, they can obstruct the flow of ch'i to your home and limit its beneficial energy. Remove dead leaves and branches from trees and shrubs near your home to prevent an image of death and decay. From a practical perspective, keeping dead limbs neatly trimmed will prevent them from falling on power lines, damaging your property, or perhaps causing an injury.

**Superimpose the bagua over your yard.**

Place the eight-sided bagua over a plot plan or sketch of your property, just as you did with the floor plan of your home's interior. Align the arrow at the center of the yard's border that bears the driveway, sidewalk, or entrance to your property. Now you can see which areas of your yard correspond to which parts of your life. (See chapter 3 for a diagram of the bagua.)

## Weed your garden.

Weeds suggest that problems are choking your personal growth and limiting your good fortune. Pull them out to remove impediments to your happiness. Weeds also obscure flowers and deprive them of nutrients—get rid of them so you can showcase your favorite plants.

## Organize garden tools.

Store small tools in a bucket or basket with a handle. This keeps them together and makes them easy to transport.

## Cut the grass.

Neatly trimmed grass adds to your home's visual appeal and attracts positive ch'i. An overgrown yard symbolizes tasks or problems that are growing out of control. Keep grass neatly trimmed to get a handle on challenges in your life and to present a positive image to passersby.

## Rake your yard.

This uncluttering cure improves the outer appearance of your home and makes it more attractive to visitors and ch'i. Because fallen leaves symbolize death and decay, it's a good idea to promptly remove them from your yard.

## Fill in a missing gua with symbolic corners.

If your home is missing a gua, fill in the gap with a symbolic corner outside (see chapter 3 for more information). Place an object—a plant, flagpole, light, birdbath, or wind chime, for instance—where the missing corner *would* be positioned if you visually extended the walls of your house.

## Eliminate straight lines and sharp angles in a garden.

Gardens are oases where we go to find peace and relaxation. Straight lines and sharp angles, however, symbolize rapid movement and activity and can produce stress instead of tranquility. Nature doesn't usually form straight lines or right angles—follow her lead and design your garden with graceful curves.

### Stack wood to encourage growth.

In feng shui, wood symbolizes growth and expansion. If you use wood in a fireplace, woodstove, or fire pit, stack it neatly in the gua that represents an area of your life in which you want growth to occur.

### Make a statement in your Self/Identity Gua.

Clear away anything in your Self/Identity Gua that doesn't represent you. Then make this area as distinctive and beautiful as possible—plant flowers, install attractive lighting, etc. If your mailbox is in this gua, decorate it with positive images from your life (for example, if you enjoy sailing, paint boats on it). If your front door falls in your Self Gua, paint it a bright, cheerful color (red is considered lucky in feng shui) and affix handsome brass numerals to the door.

### Clean gutters.

Clogged gutters symbolize stagnant conditions and obstructions in your life. Unblock gutters so water—and ch'i—can flow freely.

### Organize a neighborhood cleanup project.

Get neighbors together to clean up litter and natural debris in your area. A group endeavor not only makes the work go quicker, it gives you an opportunity to strengthen relationships with neighbors and demonstrate pride in your community.

**Put a recycling bin near mailboxes in an apartment building.**
If you live in an apartment building, you can keep fliers and junk mail
from accumulating and cluttering the entryway to your building by setting
a recycling bin near the mailboxes. This cure makes it easy for residents to
discard junk mail and other unwanted paper.

**Use the bagua to analyze an apartment building.**
If you live in an apartment building, position the bagua over a plan of the
entire building by aligning the arrow with the main entrance. Although
your own apartment has a more direct influence on your life than the
common areas, the building in which you live will also affect you. For
instance, cleaning up the entrance to your apartment building can help
prevent problems with neighbors and present a positive image to passersby.

### Replace burned-out lights.

From a practical perspective, good lighting outside your home allows you and your visitors to see clearly and prevents accidents. In feng shui, light symbolizes the sun's life-giving energy. Replace burned-out lights, especially at the entrance to your home, to attract ch'i and its benefits.

### Move noisy objects out of the Relationships Gua of your property.

Noisy objects and equipment, such as lawnmowers and power saws, can cause friction between you and a partner if you store them in the Relationships Gua of your property. Move them to another location.

### Clean out your garage.

Like other uncluttering cures, this one helps you to eliminate confusion, obstacles, and old behavior patterns and habits. It also clears the way for new opportunities and good luck to enter your life. Break this task down into manageable components so you don't become overwhelmed—or get the whole family involved.

### Pay attention to the location of garbage cans.

Trash represents things in your life that you are ready to release. Notice which gua your garbage can occupies. If it is located in your Wealth Gua, you may be throwing away your money. If you put it in your Relationships Gua, you could be dumping garbage into your love life.

**Clean out your car, including the trunk and glove compartment.**
Clutter in your car can cause confusion, delays, obstacles, and other
problems when you travel. Clean your car, inside and out, to facilitate
both local and long-distance trips. This also helps you find important
materials (such as your registration) and safety equipment (flashlight, tire
gauge, ice scraper, etc.) when you need them. The more time you spend in
your car, the more important this cure is.

### Smudge your car's interior.

Perform this cure any time you feel a need to disperse disruptive energies from your car, such as after a particularly stressful trip or an accident. It's a good idea to smudge a car when you buy it, too, especially if someone else owned it previously, to remove other people's vibes. Burn sage or pine incense—you can use the ashtray, if there is one—to clear away unwanted energies and purify the interior of your vehicle.

### Use a net or screen to organize your trunk.

Nets or screens designed to fasten in your trunk keep stuff from sliding around when you drive. They also compartmentalize and keep handy tools, supplies, and other gear that permanently reside in your trunk.

### Have a space for trash in your car.

Have a designated place for receipts, wrappers, and other trash in your car—and use it. Empty it daily to keep clutter from accumulating.

### Organize loose change.

If you use coins for tolls, parking meters, or car washes, use a coin holder in your car to organize loose change and keep it handy.

### Use pet guards in your car.

Allowing pets to jump around in the car while you drive is dangerous—for them and for you. If you regularly travel with pets, keep them safely restrained and away from the driver by installing pet guards. Use carrying cages with attached food and water dishes for short or occasional trips.

### Hang a wind chime between your home and electrical power lines.

To counteract the unwanted effects of electromagnetic frequencies (EMFs) from power lines, hang a wind chime between your home and the electrical lines. This cure disperses stress-producing EMFs that can clutter your environment and circulates them away from your home.

### Hang a wind chime between your home and a noisy neighbor.

A wind chime can also disperse the disruptive influence of a noisy neighbor. Hang one between your home and theirs to chase away atmospheric clutter and its disturbing effects.

### Hang a bagua on a door that faces a busy street.

If you live on a busy or noisy street, hang a bagua on the door facing the street to reflect noise and disruptive energy away from your home. This cure helps prevent atmospheric clutter and the resulting stress from adversely impacting the inhabitants of your home.

### Bury money to attract prosperity.

Fill a small, rectangular cardboard box with coins and tie a red ribbon around it. (Rectangles symbolize growth; red is a lucky color in feng shui). Then "plant" the box by burying it in the Wealth Gua of your property to attract prosperity.

### Encourage kids to pick up toys.

Toys strewn about the yard, porch, or driveway create an unsightly appearance that symbolizes confusion and carelessness. In some cases, scattered toys may even cause accidents. Encourage children to pick up their toys after they've finished using them.

### Arrange patio furniture outside to fill in a missing gua in your home.

You can compensate for a missing gua in your home's floor plan by arranging patio furniture outside the house, in the space where the missing sector should be. This cure visually extends the footprint of your home and invites activity into the part of your life represented by that gua.

### Hang prayer flags to promote peace.

Buddhists traditionally hang colorful flags printed with prayers and blessings outside their homes and temples. When the wind blows, it carries the blessings to other beings around the world. You can write your own good wishes on colorful pieces of cloth and tie them to a pole, tree, clothesline, etc., to promote peaceful, positive conditions in your environment.

CH

7

# CLUTTER CONTROL
# FOR KIDS

### Get kids involved in clutter control.

Encourage children to unclutter their rooms. Clutter in children's bedrooms can increase restlessness, distraction, frustration, and confusion. It also puts obstacles in their way. "A chaotic sea of stuff and inappropriate storage options can disrupt children's lives at every stage of development," explains Lisa Skolnik in her book *The Right Storage.* Toy chests, shelves, baskets, colorful plastic tubs, etc., make it easy for them to put away games and toys after playing with them. Help kids appreciate the value of putting their stuff away so they can find it the next time they want it.

### Don't let kids think you'll do everything for them.

Get kids in the habit of picking up after themselves from an early age, so they don't expect you to do it for them (or others later on in life). Organizing personal belongings has a direct relationship to organizing thoughts, and being used to tidying up improves a child's ability to think clearly and logically. Studies suggest that children who grow up in neat, orderly environments tend to do better in school and be more successful as adults.

### Give kids their own bulletin boards.

Clean clutter off your refrigerator door by giving kids personal bulletin boards for displaying their artwork, class schedules, reading lists, souvenir photos, after-school activities info, and so on. Hang the bulletin boards in their bedrooms to help them organize their lives and celebrate themselves at the same time.

**Place books in the Knowledge Gua of a child's room.**
Neatly organizing books in this sector of a child's bedroom encourages learning and can improve his or her schoolwork.

**Keep screens out of the Knowledge Gua of a child's playroom or study room.**
If you place a TV or computer in the Wisdom/Knowledge Gua of a child's room, you encourage him or her to glean too much information from this single source. Instead, organize books, encyclopedias, atlases, and a variety of other learning tools in this sector to stimulate intellectual growth. (Also, as for adults, it's best to keep screens out of sleeping spaces altogether.)

### Collect bath toys in a basket beside the tub.

Rather than allowing toys to remain in the tub—or on the floor—after bath time, corral them neatly in a basket or colorful plastic bin beside the tub.

### Recycle kids' toys.

When children outgrow their toys, pass them on to friends' younger children or donate them to charity. Holding on to outdated objects shows a reluctance to release the past and embrace the future.

## Keep toy collections from growing out of control.

Each time a child receives a new toy, instruct him or her to give away an old one. Let the child decide whether to give an outgrown toy to a friend, younger sibling, or charity. This cure not only keeps toy collections from expanding ad infinitum, it encourages kids to share with others.

## Nab toys left lying around the house or yard.

If kids neglect to pick up toys and put them away after playing with them, collect errant toys and hold them for ransom. Children can reclaim their toys by doing extra chores or other good deeds. If a child doesn't miss a toy you've confiscated after a period of time, give it away. He or she probably doesn't need it.

## Remove articles that symbolize conflict from the Helpful People Gua of a child's room.

The symbolism associated with war-oriented video games, toy soldiers, action hero dolls, play guns, etc., can have a destructive effect on a child's relationships with other kids. If your child plays with toys that have potentially violent associations, move these from the Helpful People Gua, which relates to friendship. This cure discourages conflict and encourages cooperation and congeniality between children—it can also help a child make new friends.

## Let kids hold a mini yard sale.

Kids can have fun and earn extra money by holding their own mini yard sale. Encourage young entrepreneurs to sell toys they no longer play with. Cleaning their rooms becomes fun when they can turn their own clutter into cash.

**Furnish children's rooms with easily accessible storage pieces.**
Adult-size dressers and chests of drawers may be too tall for young children to access conveniently. Low-to-the-floor chests of drawers, trunks, and beds with integrated shelves or storage drawers underneath the mattress are easier for them to reach.

**Install a pegboard or hooks in children's rooms.**
Closet bars are often too high for young children to reach and can discourage neatness. Make it easy for kids to hang up their clothes by installing a pegboard or hooks at a convenient height. If possible, lower clothing rods so they are more convenient.

**Buy kid-sized hangers for children.**
Standard hangers are too big for children's clothing. Buy kid-sized hangers that are scaled down to fit their clothes—and colorful plastic ones are more fun to use than conventional wire hangers.

**Give children their own clothes hampers.**
Brightly colored plastic bins or cloth hampers in whimsical shapes designed to hang on the back of a closet door can inspire kids to pick up their dirty clothes. When they change clothes, they can immediately toss dirty ones into their very own laundry baskets. This can also make it easier for you to organize dirty laundry on wash day.

**Simplify bed making for kids.**

Buy bedding that makes it quick and easy for kids to make their own beds—the fewer layers, the better. If you let kids choose their own colorful, whimsical, or hobby-oriented bedding, they'll be more likely to make their beds.

### Give each child towels of a different color.

Cut down on laundry by assigning each child a towel color of his or her own choosing. Give each child two towels in his or her special color. Then make them responsible for keeping track of their towels, hanging them up, and putting them in the laundry basket.

### Let kids choose household chores.

Like adults, kids may prefer to do some household chores rather than others. If there are several children in the family, allow them to work out with their siblings who will do what, so that everyone assumes his or her fair share.

### Rotate children's chores.

Allowing children to rotate their chores on a weekly basis encourages them to master a variety of tasks while also reducing the boredom factor.

### Improve a child's dusting skill.

To make sure a child dusts all those nooks and crannies, hide loose change in often-missed spots. The more effective the duster is, the more money he or she will make.

## Curb overstimulation.

Objects that represent the fire element—TVs, computers, red- or orange-colored objects, action toys—stimulate activity, individuality, and vitality. But too much of this element can cause restlessness and stress. Reduce the number of fire items in a child's room to tone down the tension surrounding him or her. Articles that embody the earth and metal elements can also help offset fire's influence and promote stability—see chapter 3 for more information.

## Limit children's activities.

Many children are involved in so many activities—sports, music lessons, dance classes, etc.—that they have little downtime. Overbooking a child's schedule can clutter their lives and yours, creating stress for everyone. Determine which activities are most important and eliminate the others.

## Limit screen time.

Often, TV, the internet, and video games become "babysitters" for kids. Devoting too much time to these activities can interfere with a child's creative development, and studies also show that obesity is increasing among today's kids because they are too sedentary. Limit the amount of time kids spend in front of screens and encourage them to pursue other interests and activities instead.

**Arrange three items that signify positive goals in the Future Gua of a child's room.**

Three is the number of growth and putting ideas into action. Choose three objects that symbolize positive goals and accomplishment—sports trophies, blue ribbons, diplomas, a telescope, painting supplies, or a chemistry set, for example. Display these neatly in the Future Gua of the child's room to encourage success and achievement.

**Give children their own workstations.**

To help kids keep their schoolwork in order and encourage learning, provide each child with his or her own desk, chair, lamp, and bookcase. If possible, place these in the Knowledge Gua of the child's room (or the room where he or she does homework).

**Strengthen a child's sense of self.**

Arrange nine items that a child particularly likes and that represent positive goals or ideals in the Self/Identity Gua of his or her room.

**Allow each child one idiosyncratic collection they never have to prune.**

While encouraging children to be neat and orderly by reducing clutter in other areas of their lives, allow them to have one special collection that they never have to prune. For one child, this might be a collection of stuffed animals; others might collect rocks or baseball cards or toy cars. Stipulate that they must keep their collections organized and contained within their own rooms (or another designated spot), rather than allowing these to overflow into the rest of the home.

CH

8

# CONTROL CLUTTER IN YOUR PERSONAL LIFE

### Do one thing at a time.

Instead of multitasking, focus on one task at a time and devote yourself to it completely. When you try to do several things at once, you may not be able to pay attention to—or enjoy—any of them fully. Confusion, stress, and forgetfulness can result.

### Meditate regularly.

Many spiritual and healing traditions recommend daily meditation as a way to clear the mind and balance emotions. Just ten minutes a day can reduce stress, help center your mind, and increase your sense of well-being. Set aside a brief period every day (preferably the same time each day) to meditate or to simply sit quietly—think of this as your personal uncluttering time.

### Establish a personal centering ritual.

We all engage in rituals, from simple routine activities such as a morning coffee break to observing holiday traditions. Rituals serve as guideposts and centering devices that help us establish a sense of order in our lives. Create a daily personal centering ritual to calm the mind and balance emotions; for example, burn incense, go for a walk, or take a relaxing bath before bed.

**Read inspirational literature.**

Begin each day by reading something inspirational—the *I Ching*, poetry by Rumi, or a religious text, for instance. This morning ritual helps to clear the mind of negativity and provides nourishing food for thought throughout the day.

**Ring a bell to focus your mind.**

Ring a bell or chime whenever you begin to feel scattered, stressed, or tired. The pleasing sound will focus your mind and bring you back to the present. Ringing bells and chimes also breaks up and disperses atmospheric clutter that can produce tension in your environment.

**Make lists.**

It's difficult and stressful to try to remember all the things you need to do. Keep lots of lists, so you don't forget something important. Use a bullet journal, if that works well for you, or neatly organize items in a notebook or a loose-leaf binder that lets you remove or add pages as needed. Crossing off completed tasks adds to your sense of accomplishment.

**Prioritize daily tasks.**

Rank the items on your to-do list according to their importance or urgency. Take care of the first three—or more, if possible—so that at the end of the day you'll know you've accomplished something.

**Organize your schedule to suit your own rhythms.**

Some of us are morning people, others are night people. We all have our own circadian rhythms and tend to function more effectively when we pay attention to them. Organize your schedule to coincide with your own cycles. Try to undertake challenging tasks or those that require you to be mentally sharp during your peak-performance periods. Save less demanding ones for downtimes. (Pay attention to your biorhythms, too. These operate on a more or less monthly basis—half of the time you are in an upswing period, the other half you are on the downswing. Track these and try to plan your activities accordingly.)

### Keep a notepad beside your bed.

Many people wake up in the middle of the night thinking about all the things they have to do the next day. Rather than trying to remember everything, jot them down on a handy notepad—don't use your smartphone, which gives off blue light that can disrupt your sleep. You may want to note your dreams here, too, so you don't forget them in the morning; dreams offer guidance and advice for solving problems during our waking hours.

### Keep a journal.

Rather than running thoughts and impressions through your mind, record them in a journal. This reduces mental clutter and sparks further insights. Keeping a journal is a good way to log your personal growth experiences and work through problems, too.

## Unclutter your diet.

Most of us could benefit from a little dietary uncluttering. Eliminate junk food and seek out healthier meals—you'll feel better and look better, too. You'll also save money.

## Think positive thoughts while you cook.

Your intention is the most important part of feng shui. Your thoughts and feelings are absorbed by the food you prepare, so when you eat it you take those thoughts and emotions into your body. You can actually "feed" yourself nourishing thoughts if you focus on upbeat, positive images while cooking.

## Ring a dinner gong before eating.

In some households, gongs are sometimes rung before meals to chase away unwanted energies and clear psychological clutter so those dining can eat in peace and harmony. The sound of a gong can also serve as a trigger to stimulate the appetite if the practice is done consistently, as Pavlov famously demonstrated with his dogs, and is said to improve digestion.

## No phones or TV at the dinner table.

The TV is a regular guest at many dinner tables; at others, people may be taking constant peeks at their phones. Instead of watching the news or checking the latest social media posts while you eat, focus on your dining companions to improve relationships with family members and friends. Having your attention drawn away by screens clutters your mind with thoughts that can interfere with good digestion.

**Carry on one conversation at a time.**

"Conversation clutter" occurs when we try to talk to several people at a time, interrupting each other and jumping from one conversation to another. This prevents us from giving our full attention to anyone and may cause confusion or misunderstanding. It can also show a lack of respect for the speaker. Conducting a single conversation that involves all the members of a group encourages togetherness and enables you discuss a subject with greater depth and clarity.

**Turn off the screens.**

Screens, from our phones and computers to our TVs, have become an omnipresent force in our homes and workplaces, bombarding us with images and noise. There are some we can't control, like electronic billboards and screens in bars, but that makes it even more important to control the ones we can. Keep the TV off unless you really want to view something you consider worthwhile; limit your total viewing time, and don't leave the TV on as background noise, where it will still influence you at a subconscious level. Be mindful of how much time you spend on your computer, even if it's part of your job, and don't keep your phone on you every minute of the day—try leaving it at home and going for a walk.

### Avoid constructing "what if" scenarios.

Stop cluttering your mind with all sorts of fantasy scenarios that could, perhaps, occur in the future—none of these may ever actually come to pass. Weaving endless "what if" possibilities is both tiring and unproductive. Reel in those restless thoughts, discipline your mind, and focus on the present instead. Most of all, stop worrying about things you can't do anything about anyway and turn your attention to handling the ones you can.

### Fight fair.

Arguments with people close to you are probably inevitable, but you can minimize the amount of hurt or anger generated in a heated discussion if you fight fair. Don't intentionally say things to insult, demean, or wound someone else. Try not to let an argument escalate out of control by fanning the flames. Strive for win–win solutions, rather than attempting to get the better of another person.

### Stick to the issues in an argument.

Often, we bring extraneous issues or old grievances into an argument. Instead of resolving matters, this can clutter a discussion and distract you from the main points. Stick to your primary concern and don't let yourself or others get sidetracked.

**Pay bills as soon as they arrive whenever possible.**

Bills that languish unpaid are nagging reminders of debt and lack. Pay them promptly—or set up automatic billing—so they don't dam the flow of prosperity. You'll also avoid late charges and interest. If there are bills you can't pay right away, file them according to the date due; this prioritizes debts and keeps you from accidentally missing a payment date.

**Keep track of spending.**

By being conscious of how much you're spending each week or each month and on what expenses, you show a willingness to take charge of your finances—and, on a psychological level, you encourage prosperity. If you keep careful watch on your online accounts, you might even discover an error in your favor!

### Clean out your bag or wallet.

Remove clutter from your purse and/or wallet to make room for new
money to come your way. Get rid of expired coupons, keys you don't use,
old cosmetics—everything you no longer need. Put loose change in your
money jar.

### Organize paper money by denomination.

Arranging bills by denomination in your wallet makes it easy to see
how much cash you have. It also lets you pull out the right bill and can
prevent mistakes.

### Reduce credit card clutter.

Do you have credit cards you rarely use? The more credit cards you have, the
greater are your chances of losing a card, having one stolen, or becoming
the victim of credit card fraud. Though canceling credit cards can impact
your credit rating, at the very least, cut up credit cards you don't use.

### Use calming scents to reduce stress.

Burn incense to remove disruptive ambient energies and bad vibes that can disturb your emotional or mental harmony. Incense burning can also be a valuable adjunct to meditation and other rituals. According to aromatherapy principles, calming scents such as lavender, vanilla, and sweet orange trigger the limbic system in the brain and can actually reduce mental clutter and encourage serenity.

### Use stimulating scents to enhance clarity and memory.

Burn mint- or citrus-scented incense to cleanse your mind of mental clutter. As aromatherapy has shown, these invigorating fragrances enable you to think more clearly and remember more of what you read or hear.

### Clear your Health Gua to promote well-being.

The center of your home is connected with your health. Clutter or obstacles in this area can lead to physical problems or exacerbate existing conditions. Broken or damaged objects in your Health Gua may symbolize physical impairments—fix them or get rid of them. Keep this area clean and in good repair to promote overall well-being. It's also a great idea to place something in your Health Gua that symbolizes vitality to you, such as a live plant.

### Don't entertain negative thoughts.

Focusing on negative thoughts can make you feel discouraged, tense, or powerless. Dwelling on unpleasant things may also magnify their significance in your life or give them more importance than they deserve. When negative thoughts pop into your head—especially ones concerning things you can't do anything about—push them aside and turn your attention to more positive matters.

### Delegate responsibilities to others.

Don't try to do everything yourself, even if you think you can handle tasks better than anyone else. Allow family members—especially children—to share the chores and responsibilities. This encourages them to feel more mature by taking on a larger role in the operation of the household. It can also reduce the clutter of duties and obligations in your daily life.

### Don't drive kids everywhere they want to go.

Obesity is increasing among children, and one of the reasons is they don't get enough exercise. Whenever possible, encourage them to walk or ride bicycles to school, activities, and friends' homes. When that isn't feasible, carpool. Get them to plan ahead and coordinate their schedules so you don't clutter up your day making numerous trips, or, if they're old enough, let them take public transportation to gain a sense of independence.

### Read romantic poetry to improve your love life.

Before going to sleep, read a romantic poem. This cure helps to reduce mental clutter and focuses your mind on the goal of improving your love life. Sweet dreams!

### Write a letter to someone you've been meaning to contact.

Receiving a letter from someone you haven't heard from in a while can brighten your day. Make someone else's day by writing a letter or sending an email. From the perspective of feng shui, putting things off delays good fortune and can interfere with your sense of accomplishment. This cure helps to unclutter your mind by removing an item from your to-do list.

### Set aside family togetherness time.

We tend to involve ourselves in so many outside activities that we may overlook the importance of spending time with loved ones and family members. Schedule time for family togetherness, just as you would book any other type of appointment. Shared family time should involve all members and engage everyone in positive personal interactions—watching TV and similar passive diversions don't count. Take turns deciding what you will do together as a family.

## Make a will.

None of us wants to think we're going to die, but the reality is that we all will. Make it easy for your loved ones to disperse your treasures—and get rid of any clutter you leave behind—by clearly specifying who gets what and how your affairs are to be handled after your passing. A will can help relieve confusion, guilt, and stress during a time when grief may add to the difficulty of making important decisions.

## Assess your expectations of others.

Take a good, hard look at what you expect of other people and why. Are your expectations fair and realistic? Who are they intended to benefit? What point or result do you expect as an outcome? Sometimes so-called good intentions may be misdirected, such as when you encourage a child to take music lessons because you always wanted to play the piano or pressure a partner to climb the corporate ladder because you desire status. Some expectations may be reasonable and warranted, others may create emotional clutter for the people we care about.

### Assess other people's expectations of you.

Are other people cluttering your life with their expectations? Do relatives expect you to spend every holiday with them? Does a partner expect you to handle most of the child care? Do friends drop by unannounced and expect you to entertain them? Determine which expectations are producing tension or burdening you, then work on finding constructive ways to limit unreasonable demands.

### Learn to say no.

Most of us accept invitations to events we'd rather not attend and agree to assume duties we don't want responsibility for. Instead of cluttering up your schedule with activities you find unpleasant, unrewarding, or unnecessary, learn to decline politely—without feeling guilty.

### Select your companions carefully.

Other people can take up a lot of time and emotional energy. They may even clutter your life with their problems, needs, and demands. Be selective about the people with whom you associate—weed out the ones who drain your energy, who aren't good for you, or whose company you don't particularly like. You'll have more time to enjoy the special people in your life or to do things by yourself.

### Use ribbons as reminders.

Tie ribbons in prominent places—on the kitchen faucet, your car steering wheel, your telephone receiver—to help you remember things you need to do. You may want to color-code the ribbons to provide additional information—a green ribbon on your phone might prompt you to make a doctor's appointment; a red ribbon tied around your bedpost could remind you to buy a birthday present for a significant other.

### Don't put things off.

If possible, address tasks right away rather than putting them off until some unspecified time in the future. Postponing a task not only increases the number of things you'll have to deal with later, it also produces nagging feelings of inadequacy and incompetence. Knowing a chore is looming ahead can drain your vitality and cast a shadow over your day.

### Take time out.

Give yourself a break each day to unclutter your mind and emotions. Do something you really enjoy—by yourself, for yourself—even if it's only for a few minutes. Take a hot bath, listen to relaxing music, go for a walk—whatever soothes your body and soul.

# Resources

Alexander, Skye. *10-Minute Feng Shui*. Beverly, MA: Fair Winds Press, 2019.

Kingston, Karen. *Clear Your Clutter with Feng Shui*. New York: Broadway Books, 1999.

Kondō, Marie. Trans. Cathy Hirano. *The Life-Changing Magic of Tidying Up: The Japanese Art of Decluttering and Organizing*. Berkeley, CA: Ten Speed Press, 2014.

Skolnik, Lisa. *The Right Storage: Organizing Essentials for the Home*. Gloucester, MA: Rockport Publishers, 2001.

---

# About the Author

S kye Alexander is the author of more than forty fiction and nonfiction books. Her stories have been published in anthologies internationally and her work has been translated into more than a dozen languages. She is also an artist, astrologer, tarot reader, and feng shui practitioner.

Visit her at www.skyealexander.com.

# INDEX

## A

Arguments, 195
Art of placement. *See* Feng shui
Artwork, 110, 111
Attic, 101

## B

Bagua
  about, 39
  sectors, 40–41
  using, 42–46, 128, 166
  *See also* Gua; specific Gua
Basement, 102
Bedrooms
  bell to clear air, 81
  cleaning, 78, 80
  clutter in, 80, 81
  furnishing, 78
  photographs in, 109
  remaking on laundry day, 78
  screens in, 81
Bells and chimes, ringing, 81,
  155, 189, 193
Bill paying, 196
Books, 119, 141
Borrowed items, 105
Briefcase, 146

## C

Cars, 168–169
Ceiling fans, 100
Centering rituals, 188
Chairs, 107
Ch'i, 18
Children
  activities of, 182–183
  bed making, 180
  bulletin boards for, 174
  chores, 181
  clothing care, 178
  collections of, 185
  driving places, 200
  furnishing rooms, 178
  Knowledge Gua and, 175
  personal responsibility and,
    174

towels, 181
  toys, 176–177
Children Gua. *See* Creativity/
  Children Gua
Closets
  cleaning out, 66
  closing doors, 67
  clothing rods, 67
  utilizing doors for storage, 101
Clothing
  arrangement methods, 71
  children's, 178
  color palette, 68
  disposing of, 68, 69, 70
  mending, 72
  off-season, 70
  packing, 72, 73
  shoes and socks, 75
  underwear, 72
Clutter
  activity, 29–31
  atmospheric, 35
  ch'i and, 18–19
  conversation, 194
  meanings of different types,
    25
  mental, 33–34
  new versus old, 27
  personal life and, 24–25
  relationship, 31–32
  significance of, 25–26
  workplace, 28–29, 57–59
Coat trees, 107
Cobwebs, 87
Color schemes
  for clothing, 68
  for home, 84, 85
Community Gua. *See* Family/
  Community Gua
Companions, 203
Contacts lists, 120, 130
Cooking, 193
Cosmetics, 122
Creativity/Children Gua
  about, 41
  area in home, 43
  hobby items in, 112

threes in, 112
Credit cards, 197

## D

Date books, old, 108
Decorative objects, 111
Diet, 193
Dining room table, 95
Dinner, eating, 193
Dirt, significance of, 26
Disrepair, 27

## E

Earth (element), 56
Expectations, 202–203

## F

Fame/Future Gua
  about, 41
  area in home, 43
  in children's rooms, 184
  wooden objects in, 137
  in workplace, 142, 156
Family/Community Gua
  about, 41
  area in home, 43
  encouraging unity through,
    108
  furnishings and, 84
  objects in, 108
Family time, 201
Feng shui
  about, 17
  ch'i and, 18–19
  clutter and messiness in
    personal life, 24–25
  importance of intention,
    11, 21
  objective of, 16
Fire (element), 56
Fireplaces, 99
Five elements, 55–56
Flowers, 117
Future Gua. *See* Fame/Future
  Gua